Steve Biddulph has been a psychologist and educator for over 40 years. He is this century's top-selling parenting author, with simple and accessible books in six million homes and 32 languages. Steve has toured with his live shows worldwide since the 1990s, teaching about more affectionate ways of parenting, and a more life-affirming style of masculinity.

Steve and his wife Shaaron funded the creation of the SIEVX refugee memorial on the lakeshore in Canberra, involving 300 schools and communities and over a thousand young artists. Now retired, he is involved in supporting activist mental health in the climate and environment movements, and in campaigns to lower the voting age so that younger people have a say in their own fate. Steve was voted Australian Father of the Year in 2000 and was made a Member of the Order of Australia for his work in adolescent mental health.

He describes himself today as 'coming off a low base, IQ-wise, and sinking fast' but believes his generation have a responsibility to fight for the survival of those to come, and he blogs about this in his Decade of Farewell and Wild Creature Mind online projects. See more at www.wildcreaturemind.com.

Also by Steve Biddulph

The Complete Secrets of Happy Children
The Making of Love, with Shaaron Biddulph
Manhood
Raising Boys
Raising Girls
Ten Things Girls Need Most
Fully Human

STEVE BIDDULPH

WILD CREATURE MIND

BLUEBIRD

First published in Australia 2024 by Pan Macmillan Australia

First published in the UK 2024 by Bluebird
an imprint of Pan Macmillan
The Smithson, 6 Briset Street, London EC1M 5NR
EU representative: Macmillan Publishers Ireland Ltd, 1st Floor,
The Liffey Trust Centre, 117–126 Sheriff Street Upper,
Dublin 1, D01 YC43
Associated companies throughout the world
www.panmacmillan.com

ISBN 978-1-5290-7648-6

1 3 5 7 9 8 6 4 2

A CIP catalogue record for this book is available from the British Library.

Printed and bound by CPI Group (UK) Ltd, Croydon, CR0 4YY

Visit **www.panmacmillan.com** to read more about all our books
and to buy them. You will also find features, author interviews and
news of any author events, and you can sign up for e-newsletters
so that you're always first to hear about our new releases.

You only have to let the soft animal of your body
Love what it loves.

Mary Oliver, 'Wild Geese'

Before We Begin . . .

Try this experiment.

Either out loud, or silently in your head, repeat this sentence (even though it probably isn't true): 'My life is going really well, everything is wonderful.'

Then go down into your body and notice what happens . . .?

Somewhere inside you, there will be an answer.

It will be quite subtle at first. A twinge or a stirring, or a sinking or tightening. But you felt it, didn't you? Something shadowy and faint. Something inside you has an opinion! And somehow, you know it's right.

This is your Wild Creature Mind. It knows you better than you know yourself. It's been waiting to help you since before you were born.

Say hello. You are going to make an amazing team.

Contents

Introduction

Is This You?

Let's begin with you, dear reader; we might as well cut right to the chase. Do any of the following sound like you? Or someone close to you?

- Do you have *problems with anxiety*, sometimes making it hard to go about your life, or keeping you from a good night's sleep?
- Do you have *trouble knowing your boundaries*, finding that you go along with things which betray your true self?
- Do you sometimes wonder if you even *have* a true self?
- In times when you are not stressed or anxious, does life feel rather flat and grey, and like it's *just all too hard?*
- Do *painful memories* sometimes rise up in a distressing way, making it difficult to feel happy or safe?
- Do you sometimes *question your own worth*, or worthiness of love?
- Or finally, perhaps you are in relatively good mental health, but still have grave *fears for the future of the human race*, through our terrible disconnection from each other and from the natural world?

If any of these are true for you, then first, a big hug to you. That is a hard place to be, and I have definitely been there too. Second, *you are in the right book!*

These problems are now hugely widespread, across every age group. We are especially worried about how common they are in children and teenagers. But I and many of my colleagues around the world are discovering some answers – and they come from a surprising place.

A radical understanding is emerging in mainstream neuroscience to explain our currently terrible mental health, as well as something closely related – our wider problems with living in harmony with the natural world. In a nutshell, it is this: that *we have lost touch with the animal part of our mind.* And it's a really important part – the part that helps us to let go of anxiety and be fiercely strong when we need to be. It also helps us to shake off bad memories and convert them to growth. And leads us to be more loving to ourselves and the world. To be able to 'open our hearts in hell'.

This part of our mind is the one that our ancestors (and all other animals) used for millions of years to live free and happy lives, but that we have now almost completely lost from our awareness.

This book is about how to get that part of you reactivated, to coax it out of the thickets of your mind and into the sunshine; a fierce and tender ally for life.

So, dear reader, breathe a deep breath. Feel the earth underneath you. Let your shoulders come down from around your ears. Let in the fact that someone loves you, even if they are just a shambling old psychologist on the other side of the world. We're going to get you some help.

Chapter 1

Meeting Your Other Half

A Sound in the Night

Annika woke with a start. It was the middle of the night and she'd been deeply asleep. There were muffled sounds, human sounds, coming from somewhere in the house. She stumbled out of bed and went to investigate. Then, suddenly she realised what the sound was, and her heart sank like an icy stone: *It was her daughter.*

She found fourteen-year-old Ellie lying on the cold bathroom tiles, moaning and rocking, her face and night-dress soaked with tears. Annika gathered Ellie up in her arms and held her, as her sobbing grew more desperate before slowly calming. 'It's alright, I'm here. Let it out.'

Through her tears, Ellie croaked, 'I'm sorry, Mum, I didn't want to wake you.'

Annika murmured that she would always want her to come to her, any time, day or night.

Ellie had been struggling in recent months; she'd become anxious and withdrawn, with no appetite or energy, but couldn't say why. Nothing Annika suggested seemed to help. They'd been to the doctor and talked to the school. She had suffered similar problems a few years earlier and seen a couple of different psychologists, but the problems had never really gone away.

This time they were lucky. It only took two weeks to get Ellie in to see a counsellor; they knew of families who had waited for months.

Now as Annika looked up, she could see her daughter coming out of the health centre doors and heading back to the car. Amazingly, there was a bounce in her step, and she swung easily into the passenger seat. 'Mum, she was *really nice*. Not like the other psychologists. She "gets" me.' Ellie looked different, she had some colour in her face and her eyes were bright. 'And guess what? I have a baby tiger inside me!' Annika must have looked a bit baffled. 'Don't worry – I'm not psycho! It's a *metaphor*, Mum. Well, not exactly a metaphor. I'll tell you more but first, can we go and get some food? I'm starving.'

Welcome to This Book

Dear reader. This book is bursting with stories and ideas, but every word and sentence is directed towards one single goal: to equip you and your loved ones with a life-changing skill. That skill is the ability to 'converse' with the silent half of your own brain – the right hemisphere and its vast network of nerves running through your body. Brain scientists have all kinds of technical names for this part of you, but I think you will like the one I use: I call it your Wild Creature Mind.

This is the part of our brain that our close relations – birds and animals – have used to successfully live their lives for over millions of years. It is also the part famously used by people like Albert Einstein and other breakthrough-making scientists to solve complex scientific problems. While this half of your mind is certainly ancient, it is neither primitive or simple. In fact, it is astonishingly sophisticated, as we will soon see.

The animal part of your mind is the key to good mental health because it is the 'real you' not the tangle of thinking, worry and ego that you *think* is you. It's the you you were when you were a little child, full of direct experience and wonder. It's where your empathy comes from. And also your real boundaries – your animal wisdom about what you need and don't need in your life.

Your earthiness and joy live here. Your ability to love. It's the clever part of you that reads human faces, knows who to trust. It can resolve anxiety by getting you out of your own thinking, and it has the tools to release held-in trauma – the nightmares, intrusive memories and fears affecting so many people.

I know that these sound like enormous claims, but the science is clear, and so is the word from practitioners who are teaching and using these skills around the world. After over 40 years as a therapist and a parent educator, I believe that this is a breakthrough in our long struggle to turn around our plunging mental health. And, more than that, it might transform the way that we human beings live in the world. We'll never get along well with nature, if we can't get close to our *own* nature. So much that is wrong for us – anxiety, violence, conflict and destruction – comes from having these inner storms and terrors that arise when people are out of touch with their own hearts.

Your Wild Creature Mind is like a GPS inside you, which can help guide you every day towards being truer to yourself, and more caring for other people. But first you have to re-awaken your awareness of it, and become friends. You have to build a relationship with your deeper self. That is what this book aims to teach you. The skills we will soon show you – starting in the very next chapter – are so simple you can teach them to small children. They can help a teenager's confidence or sense of direction. But they can also help old people face things that they are afraid of, and live fully to the very end. (That would be my category!)

Like any new skill (learning to swim, for instance), what we will teach you is a bit elusive to begin with, but will soon become natural and easy. (And like knowing how to swim, once you have it, you have it forever.) This skill is harder for some people than others, so we will hang in there with you and come at it from different ways until you master it.

You know how to do this. In fact, you were born doing it; you just need to remember.

By the time you finish this book, you will have the tools to inhabit your own self in a different way; a more intelligent, richer way. And that, as a poet once said, will make all the difference.

Wanted: A Big, Powerful Answer

Ellie, who we met at the start of the chapter, is just one of millions – some suggest as many as one in three of all young people today – who find the world we are living in almost impossible to bear. Parents of girls today are haunted by stories of self-harm, eating disorders and suicide attempts; they seem to be happening in every classroom, every street. Boys' problems are somewhat different, but equally problematic. (In very broad terms, girls implode, and boys explode, but there is every gradation in between.)

Many adults too – of all ages – struggle to go on with their lives. (We worry for our kids but we are not far behind.) Intergenerational trauma ripples through our families and our communities. Disillusionment and fear for the future stalk the planet. I won't swear anywhere else in this book, but it's the only word that fits here: life has become seriously f*cked.

So there is only one question that is worth asking: what do we do to fight back? How can we get the human race – and ourselves – back on track? You might be shocked to learn that some of the world's best neuroscientists think they have an answer. And it's something surprisingly simple which you, dear reader, can put into practice. With the skills you will gain as you read through this book, you can be part of turning things around.

The Astonishing Idea That We Have Two Minds

At the heart of this book is the most radical discovery in a hundred years of neuroscience and psychology. It is that our brains are divided into two halves for a reason – because, astonishing as it might sound, *we also have two minds*. And these two minds each have an entirely different way of approaching life. Successful living is a team effort between these two selves, and all animals in nature manage this routinely. But in recent centuries, we humans we have numbed out one of those halves. It has fallen silent and left us unhinged, operating with half a brain. The idea will seem bewildering at first, but as you reflect on your own experience, it will start to do what all new paradigms in science do – it will explain everything so much better. So hang in with me, dear reader. This is going to be a huge help.

What do we mean by 'two different ways of approaching life'? Well, it's like this: one of our two minds is a focused, grasping and egotistical one, living in the left hemisphere of our brain. This is the mind you are in now, as you read this book. It is good at language, fine for doing your tax, making shopping lists, building a house or organising a camping trip.

The other mind – located just a few millimetres away across a deep fissure – is your silent right hemisphere. This side of your brain is ultra-aware, receptive, socially wired and attuned to the natural world. It is designed to help us get along with each other and be at ease in our own skin. This mind operates differently to our lonely, fretting little left brain because it is not confined to inside our skull, but also includes all the nerves of our body in a continuous neural network. It is a biological system for living an attuned and wiser life.

Over recent centuries, we have lost touch with this mind, and if we are to get back on track, we need its help. Your own Wild Creature Mind has been there all your life, almost totally ignored. In fact it has become pretty cranky – and its attempts to get your attention are what make you anxious or explosive or haunted with night-mares or all the symptoms of poor mental health. But once released, it is – like any animal – forgiving and fun, full of energy and life. Depending on the situation, it can be fierce and brave. Or tender and loving. Or wildly intelligent. As you get to know your Wild Creature Mind, you will find it a delightful companion. And little by little, it will help you to unfurl your animality – to open your senses, loosen your limbs, and simply be more alive. More *here*.

The Journey We'll Go On

It's important to ground everything we have talked about in the day-to-day world, so let's go back now to Ellie.

Ellie still has a journey ahead of her before she can be completely well, but already something has shifted. She can feel it, so can her mother. So, what actually took place?

There were two ingredients in the hour and a half that Ellie spent in the health centre. One was the warmth and presence of the therapist. This woman was not a clipboard-wielding technician (of the kind that most psychology schools seem determined to turn out these days). She was more like a wise aunty who had known Ellie her whole life. Ellie felt 'held' and steadied in a way that she hadn't felt for a long time. She would later tell her father that the therapist seemed like 'the most real person I have ever met in my life'. (Her father would squirm a bit at this, wondering how he could become more 'real' for his daughter. It was a useful line of thought.)

The second thing Ellie brought out with her was something profoundly disruptive; the realisation that *she is not who she thought she was*. It is dawning on Ellie that her self-perception – which she shares with most of her generation of young people – as a broken, not-good-enough, lonely failure – is completely mistaken. She is, or has – she isn't quite sure yet which it is – *a wild animal inside her*, one which continuously shifts shape and feeling. Ellie really runs with this; she pictures her Wild Creature as somehow feline, sometimes a small cub with soft golden fur, snuggling into her for protection. And sometimes as a lithe, muscular panther, with absolute lethality in its fangs and claws, ready to protect her with its life.

It's much more than an abstract idea. Something inside has *woken up*. Her job now is to get to know it. And gradually, with its help, to track down what has harmed her so much in her short life, and to undo that harm. To do that, it will take collective action and the combined efforts of everyone around her. (We will revisit Ellie further on to see how she and her friends and family turned things around. I think you will find it stirring and helpful.)

In a nutshell, *Ellie broke free*. And in this book, we will aim to do this for you too. We will take it carefully and in small steps. We will first help you to hear the intricate signals of your Wild Creature Mind. Then we will show you how to dialogue with it and uncover the secrets it has always known about you. You will learn to use it moment by moment to feel at home in your own skin, and more effective in the world. These ideas will change in subtle but important ways how you relate to your own self and to those around you. If you struggle with self-worth and sometimes find relationships with others fraught, then this will probably help too!

We will teach you the science behind Wild Creature Mind – the simple biological fact of our two minds and how they are wired to work as a team, so you can have confidence in your own newfound abilities. We'll meet the people who discovered these ideas, and get to share in their excitement and hope. Then, to really help you bed these skills and ideas in, we will hear stories of adults and children whose lives were changed by tapping into this resource. These stories are often heartbreakingly beautiful and I hope they will stay with you forever.

Summing Up

Wild Creature Mind is the meeting point of the latest thinking in neuroscience and practical tools for using your silent animal mind. These tools are already helping thousands of people, including those who have come through terrible things – soldiers, medical staff, war zone survivors. People whom we really need to have back on their feet.

My belief is that Wild Creature Mind – the neuroscience of our right hemisphere – is a resource without equal in the often inadequate and simplistic world of mental health treatment. I hope better minds than mine will get stirred by this book and take it further. Perhaps you will be one of those.

It's a big thing to take on, a whole different way of seeing your own mind. So we are going to go carefully. In the next chapter we'll explain the biology of our two minds, so you can imagine it clearly inside your own body. Then we'll listen to your Wild Creature Mind, so you realise how you can use this every day, how you 'sort of knew but didn't know'. Your Wild Creature has been watching over you since before you were born, and it has answers to questions that have troubled you all your life. It's time you got acquainted.

Grrrrowlllll!!

The animal part of your mind is the key to good mental health because it is the 'real you'. Not the tangle of thinking, worry and ego that you think is you. It's the you you were when you were a little child, and the world was fresh and new.

Chapter 2

How Your 'Other Mind' Works and How it Talks to You

Okay, dear reader – time for some science. Nothing too difficult. And pretty amazing stuff.

Have a look at this picture, and see what you can see . . .

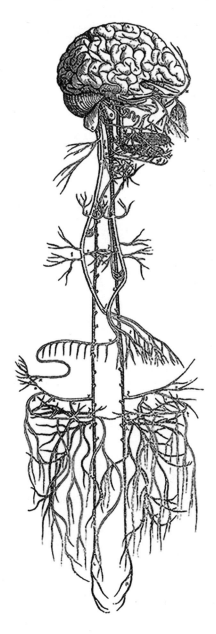

Yes, I know – ick!! It's a bit Frankenstein, but it's beautiful too. The drawing is by one of those remarkable 19th century anatomists who traced every single nerve to find out where they went and how they were connected. It shows a person seen from the front with their head turned to their left side, so you can see the right side of their brain. Out to the right, you can see where their face is, with the nerves that run into their nose and jaw. Coming down from the person's brain and into their torso is a big double nerve network. Two big branches go right down, around their heart, abdomen and pelvis.

Astonishingly, almost every nerve in this picture is part of one system – it's the vagus nerve, named after vagrant or vagabond; the 'wanderer' because, baby, it goes everywhere! And this is just *one part* of our nervous system. It doesn't include the sensory nerves running from every toe and finger and patch of skin, let alone the hormonal systems signalling to and fro, the dilating and contracting of blood vessels, the prickling of hair or twitching of muscles or the waves-crashing blossoming of reproductive organs. (Trying to be tasteful here.) Head to toe, your right brain and body are one network. So far, so good.

Now, as we've noted, the human brain, and every brain of every living creature, has a distinct feature. It is *divided*. A big gap runs down the middle, so you can actually almost separate the halves, just like you can separate an orange when you share it between two people. Below are other, more primitive structures like the limbic system, the motor cortex and so on, and these are divided as well. Nature really wanted us to have two separate brains.

The two halves are normally called 'hemispheres', so in the picture you are looking at you can only see the right hemisphere. The left hemisphere is hidden from view on the other side. The left hemisphere, the unseen one, has something very important – just above and behind where the left ear stick outs, are two areas – called Broca's region, and Wernicke's region. These two brain parts handle the *making* of language and the *understanding* of language respectively. The left side of your brain is therefore the one that 'does words'. And words go in lines (called sentences), so they manage linear thought.

So it easily follows that this left side is the part that you think is 'you' – the part that chatters and says, 'My name is . . .' and 'I was born in . . .' and 'I need to get something organised for dinner . . .' It's good for being organised, but it's also rather an exhausted, confused self, prone to getting into worry and tangled arguments in the middle of the night. It can only go in straight lines, and life often just isn't like that.

The left hemisphere's job is to be very focused. So it is wired in a way that minimises awareness of anything else – like sensory input. It is kind of a 'brain in a box', up there in its little garret, writing stories to itself. The problem is that your left hemisphere was never meant to operate on its own. It can be a wonderful tool, but for a rich, grounded, and effective life, it needs its right-brain partner; it needs your Wild Creature Mind.

The right hemisphere is far more deeply interlinked with your body. It is the first to receive most of the sensory input, including things which your left hemisphere doesn't even notice. It reads other people's faces to be able to detect their true intent, or if something is amiss, which is very important for your life to go well, whether you are raising a family or running a country. It even has nerves running into your face, showing your true intent even if you try to hide it.

The vagus nerve system going down into your torso is a double system. It sends messages like *Speed up heart*, *Slow down stomach*, and it also brings back messages from all of your inner organs, as well as muscles, skin and so on. And it is only a part of your huge sensory network going to every fingertip and toe. Eighty per cent of our nervous system is devoted to bringing information back to our brains, and especially to the right hemisphere. To your Wild Creature Mind.

Noticing Your Felt Sense

Just picture those nerve networks inside your own body. If you shift your focus of attention down inside yourself, you can even feel that aliveness there in your chest and belly, faintly glowing with life, tiny stirrings and twitches. Of course, that can include the breakfast you ate too fast; it's all part of the picture. There is always a slight movement of sensations that tells you your body is there.

That your legs are there, the top of your head is there, even though you can't see it.

And that your 'insides' are there.

But on top of that, there is *something else*. There are sensations, of tension or movement or tingling, or any one of hundreds of words you could use, which seem to be a response to what is going on inside your thoughts, or from what is happening around you. To what people say. What you see or read or think. What your environment is like. These are very subtle until you get used to attending to them, but they become clearer and they *mean something*. They are palpable, and they are significant. Your job is to pay attention, to have a curious, and in a way, respectful attitude. To make them welcome. Because this is your right hemisphere mind, trying to get through to you.

Always remember the vital fact: the right side of your brain, the smart and multitasking super-aware part, *does not have words*. Our right hemisphere cannot say 'Watch out!' or 'This doesn't add up' or 'Go for it!'. Instead, as with every other animal that ever lived, it speaks by felt sensations – down those nerves and into your body. So by going slightly quiet and paying attention, you can listen to it *right here and now*. It is like an animal guardian, a guide to everything from danger to deep love and trust. It is very worth listening to, as we are going to show you in the chapters and stories to come.

The aim of this book is to help you to do two things together – think in words, and listen to felt sense too. To get both sides of your brain onto the job of sorting out your life. Words are incredibly useful for communicating our thoughts, explaining things and being organised. But life is often more multidimensional and dynamic than words can ever encompass, and we often just have to feel our way. Sometimes, reality has to be 'danced' rather than reasoned. Words won't help you know, for example, when to be brave and when to be afraid. How to balance – day to day – being a loving parent and still keeping some sense of self. Or when is the right moment to ask for a kiss! These things have to be *felt*.

The sensations in your body are not all about digestion or too-tight undies! Along with those, there are messages from your right brain, quiet and shy, though sometimes of course, yelling at you to watch out. If you pay really close attention, you can feel those sensations *right now*, as you are reading this page – 'That feels right', 'That feels wrong'. (Or 'I need to go and pee!' – mind and body are not separate.) Your insides speak to you freshly each moment.

And if you have no idea what we are talking about here, don't worry. About one person in three is so used to

26

ignoring their inner body sensations – either from trauma, or just simply never having thought about them – that they cannot recognise them immediately. The good news is that you stand to benefit the most of any reader of this book. Help is on its way.

Summing Up

I know this is a bit mind-spinning, but we are going to set it out much more in the chapters to come. For now, just hold onto that basic fact: *you have two minds*. One of them is silent. It talks through the body, and it has important things to say. Listening to it is a skill you can acquire.

Soon we will show you how your Wild Creature side can be expressive, articulate and subtle. That little creature inside you has been shapeshifting and whispering and sometimes screaming at you all your life. In fact, many of the mental health symptoms we experience – anxiety, problems with boundaries, depression, traumatic stress, and loneliness, are actually caused by not being in touch with its 'felt sense' guidance. With our true power source. The wild animal part of you is going to be mightily pleased that you're finally ready to listen.

Sometimes, reality has to be 'danced' rather than reasoned. Words won't help you know when to be brave and when to be afraid. How to balance being a loving parent and still keeping some sense of self. Or when is the right moment to ask for a kiss! These things have to be felt.

Chapter 3

How to Hear the Voice of Your Wild Creature Mind

Without further ado, let's now experience your Wild Creature Mind talking to you. The quiet but unmistakeable signals it sends, and how fascinating and useful they are.

While going through this chapter, you will need to read more slowly, giving yourself time to immerse yourself in each step. Breathe deeply now, to break the pace of your reading, and it will be a better experience.

Okay, then we are ready to start.

AN EXERCISE IN NOTICING YOUR FELT SENSE

For this experiment, you simply choose two people that you care about. If you have kids, two of those kids would be perfect for this. No kids – you could use your two parents or two of your friends. (If you are a childless, friendless orphan, then a big hug to you – but don't worry, it can be two neighbours, movie stars or musicians. Any two people will do.) When you have chosen them, read on.

Now, pick one of those two. Child or person A. Picture them in your 'mind's eye'. Perhaps even hear their voice, or see their face. Then, as you do this, go down into your body and notice what happens, especially down the centre of your torso. What slight sensations, changes, movements or little stirrings happen in your body as you think of this person? Notice the *location* of those sensations. They might be down the middle of your body, in your heart or stomach or solar plexus or just under your skin. Somewhere – anywhere – inside you. Perhaps even in your face, throat, shoulders or head. The sensations might be quite marked or ever so slight, barely there. They might be a tightening, or an ache, a falling away or a pressure or a warming. They might be swirling or clenched. They might even be 'nothing', like a numb or empty sensation. Even 'nothing' is a sensation.

Just notice.

As you are sensing inside yourself, try to give a word or description to that sensation, to tag it in some way. If you had to tell someone else about it, how would you describe it? If you had to draw it, what would it look like? (If you are having trouble though, don't worry, we will help you as we go further. Your Wild Creature has been used to hiding, it might not show up right away! Be patient, and gentle and it will emerge.) Feel it, locate it and describe it. That's all you have to do.

Now, whether or not you have much to report, go to the other person you chose. The other child, or friend or parent or neighbour, and do the same thing. Picture them, think of them and as you do that, go down inside yourself again, and notice if your body reacts and how. Notice if it is different to the first person. What feelings happen down the midline of your body, or elsewhere? Even the slightest stirrings or tensing, or falling away. Again, if you can, give it a few words of description, or picture it or imagine how you might describe it to someone else. 'When I thought of my oldest boy, my body kind of . . .'

Okay, now, let's leave that. Let's go back to our 'thinking minds' and reflect a little.

What is going on here? The two people you chose 'matter' to you, they occupy space in your mind and are possibly very consequential. (If they are your children, you may feel that their lives are more important to you than your own.) But what you are noticing is that their significance isn't just an abstract idea. Thinking of these people will literally move you – you can feel it in your body. There is a 'felt sense' inside you, associated with this person, right now, as you think of them. It is giving you an up-to-the-minute executive memo about where you are at with this person. And that sensation is a *living, changing thing.*

For example, if you chose one of your children, your felt sense of them is a composite totality of your relationship with them *right now.* Perhaps you argued with them this morning, or something about them has been concerning you. 'Right nowness' is the key feature of felt sense. And it is lightning fast – did you notice how those sensations were immediate? Before you really had a chance to do any more than think 'oldest boy', the body change was there? It was instant, and it was fresh. Felt sense is never the same two times in a row. Were you to have done this exercise yesterday, it would have been different. Like the ocean or the sky, felt sense changes moment by moment. And as we will discover, that changeable quality of the felt sense is the key to using it in healing, since when we attend to and talk to it, it will update and improve. It is there to tell you something, and when you finally listen, *its job will be done and it will quieten and be at peace.*

What if My Wild Creature is Scary?

The felt sense can be ever-so-subtle or almost violently strong. A friend of mine's teenage daughter survived an horrific trauma and when he did this exercise about a year later, thinking of her, his arms and hands felt so charged with energy that they rose up in front of him. His whole felt sense was protective and, quite possibly, enraged. Having this known and out in the open was helpful for him.

For many people, the felt sense can be so ever-present that it feels like normal, so it takes a little longer to tune into what it wants. Many children of Holocaust survivors, for example, have described having tight shoulders or compressed shallow breathing all their lives. They are shocked to learn that this can be different. My parents were teenagers during the Blitz – the intense bombing of British cities during World War Two. They in turn had fathers who had fought in World War One, so their history just rolled back into endless trauma, as it still does for millions of people. Held-in patterns of breathing, limits on emotionality, hyper-vigilance or anxiety were soaked into their lives.

Mum and Dad were gentle, which I am so grateful for, but they were also incredibly muted and shy. They had no idea what to do with emotions. Here is a rather sharp example. From boyhood, my dad had been keen on photography. But even into his fifties he'd never owned more than a point and shoot camera. I knew that the camera of his dreams was a Pentax SLR. So, with my first month's pay-packet, I got him a good but second-hand one, which someone I knew had for sale. When he opened the birthday present, he was so struck by the size of the gift, but could not contain that much feeling in his English heart. So instead of 'Thank you!' he muttered something about 'How could you afford this?' *And that was it.* I'd planned this as a lovely moment, for months, a thank you from a son to his dad. He was dazed, I was hurt, and nothing more was ever said. People were very messed up in those days. No wonder I wrote a bestseller about men and their emotions!

It takes a bit of work to escape our childhoods. In intensive group therapy as part of my training, in my late twenties, I relearned how to cry after not having done so since about the age of four. I also uncovered volcanic amounts of rage, the strength of which really shocked me. (I don't think this is unusual in people from Western backgrounds, where emotional suppression is simply the cultural norm.) Grief educator Elisabeth Kübler-Ross used a big red mattress in the centre of the room for people to beat on in order to release the intense anger they might have about grief and loss they were facing. Your Wild Creature comes out when it's safe and, paradoxically, letting it out in safe ways makes us so much less explosive. We can release it one shudder at a time! Even if we just allow it to be present in our body a little, as a felt sense, and breathe through it, but not push it away, then we are on our way.

Ann Weiser Cornell, a pioneer in using body awareness to release trauma gently, suggests you also get in touch with your fear of your emotions and focus on that, noticing how *that* feels. By giving it some acceptance, it often will diminish a little. We often have deep beliefs held in our body – 'If I cry, I will never stop', or 'If I get angry, I will annihilate the whole world'. In childhood, we might have concluded that from the behaviours of those around us. But really, they are just feelings and can be managed quite safely simply by letting them run through our body with a therapist's support, or our own gentle acceptance.

Every honestly felt flash of anger or grief allowed through our body is a step towards being healed and integrated. We should respect the scale of what we are addressing, and give it time to happen.

Sometimes, these problems have been passed down for thousands of years. How wonderful that we might be the ones to break those chains.

Felt Sense is Not the Same as Feelings

After doing the 'two people' experiment, you might well say, 'Of course I have feelings about my children, different feelings – what is surprising about that?' And while this is true, we are talking about something quite different, the sensations that happen 'down further', and which precede emotions. These are much more valuable in finding your way. If you 'always' feel angry, or 'always' end up feeling sad, then going down deeper into the sensations is going to really help you get unstuck.

In our culture, we use the words 'feelings' or 'emotions' to denote general categories of bodily reaction and the thoughts that go with them. Anger, fear, sadness and joy – the four primary emotions – are almost like points of the social compass, and hugely important in guiding our lives. But they are also prone to a lot of error. In the therapy world, having once strongly advocated tracking down your real feelings, we are now beginning to realise that they are secondary products of a deeper process – and that it is the underlying bodily sensations that precede them which are the most useful thing to focus on. Our emotions can be

37

hijacked by the social environment around us; think of the massive addiction to outrage that has happened in the age of social media.

Renowned brain researcher Professor Lisa Feldman Barrett was one of the first to explain how feelings arise not from conscious thought but from sensations – from the Wild Creature side. This went right against the idea prevalent in 20th century psychology, that we create emotions with our thinking. Lisa writes, 'We don't cry because we are sad. It's the other way around. *We know we are sad, because we are crying.*' You only have to reflect on your experience of this to know that it's true. We know we are angry because we are hot and tense. Scared, because we are shaking. Happy, because we feel like jumping up and down!

Our Wild Creature Mind sends these messages to our body because it wants us to notice and respond. When a little child says they have a big black feeling in their tummy, sit with them quietly and ask them 'What do you think that feeling is wanting to say to you?' (In Chapter 10, we'll teach you how to use felt sense with children, along with some great stories of parents doing just that.)

Felt sense is the tip of an iceberg of *meaning* waiting for you to come and explore. I can't emphasise this enough – it *knows things*. It comes from somewhere deep in your right hemisphere, where complex matters are managed, the kind of matters that no mere line of thought could properly deal with, and certainly not at the speed that life often requires. At those times when you know you have over-reacted, or felt upset beyond what seemed proportionate, you can use those body signals, and by sitting quietly with them, figure out – what *was* going on for me there? What did that experience *mean*? If you are patient enough, the answers will come.

When you did the exercise and noticed some body sensations associated with the people you thought of, it's quite likely that you also experienced a curiosity or urge to follow up those body sensations, to 'get to the bottom of them'. This is what your Wild Creature invites, and in fact is there for; to help us have *new* thoughts. Our right hemisphere is always wanting to lead us to the edge of what is happening right now. It is our inner therapist, saying, 'Pay attention. Something here is important.'

Human beings are designed to progress and grow – wiser, more loving, more alive. We have an inbuilt momentum, just as a tree wants to go 'up', we want to go 'forward' in our lives, to learn and explore. It hurts to be blocked, or going in circles. In fact, this is the heart of despair – the pain we feel to not have a way forward.

Our Wild Creature Mind activates most strongly, and comes to our help, when we have got stuck in some way. It has something to say which we *really* need to know. Not to necessarily *obey*, but to take account of, and integrate, in order to be unified and strong. In Chapter 6, we will take this to the next step – how to dialogue with your felt sense in order to uncover the story it is trying to tell you – but let's not get ahead of ourselves! Breathe deep and slow. We will take it slowly, so your left brain is happy too. We have barely scratched the surface yet. The best is yet to come.

WHY CBT OFTEN DOESN'T HELP

For the last twenty years, going to a psychologist almost always meant being treated with something called Cognitive Behavioural Therapy or CBT for short. CBT is based on the idea that poor thinking is the cause of many of our mental health problems. By the therapist challenging unhelpful thoughts or attitudes, the patient will see the sense of this and get well. (I know, it's so lightweight that it might blow away, but there you go.) Unsurprisingly, the experience of people getting help of this kind was often very mixed. Advocates of CBT have gradually begun to admit that it often fails because it disregards the natural way the brain is wired; that you cannot force feelings to change. Patients often tell me they simply felt disrespected, especially when the therapist was half their age and had not lost a child, or been widowed young or seen comrades blown to pieces in a combat zone, but was telling them that 'their feelings did not make sense'. CBT *can* be helpful, but without addressing and respecting the felt sense drivers below our thoughts it can just make matters worse.

Like all therapies, the personal qualities of the therapist are the real determinants of success. (We have actually known this since the 1960s.) If a therapist is genuinely caring, is respectful, honest and regards you as an equal, then the methods or approach used are almost irrelevant. Too many times I have listened to teenagers or adults who said, 'I felt I was just ticking boxes' or 'I was just another unit to be put through a process'. But for every one of these, I heard, 'Yes, I felt they cared about me, and they were treating me as an individual.' So, if seeking a therapist, I would recommend you always have a trial session and listen to your Wild Creature Mind, which is very good at sensing the safe from the superficial. A good therapist will be comfortable with you auditioning them to see if there is a fit, and won't be upset if you don't go ahead.

All the great swag of therapies that have come in recent years, with their various acronyms (DBT, EFT, EMDR), have sought to fill the gaps, and each offers both a promise – of new scope – and a danger – of formulaic processing of a person instead of the formation of a bond with them. Therapy must be relational, and that means doing more than applying a method. Once trust is real, then all of these can be of great help.

Our right hemisphere knows when it is being gamed. People who are in a terrible place deserve their therapist's full humanity, to know they are really there for them, rather than hiding behind some manual to mask their limitations.

As I taught my trainees over many years, the intensity of our *caring* has to match the intensity with which our patients were *harmed* in the first place. And that is helped when both therapist and client can drop their masks and the Wild Creature Mind is safe to emerge. Healing can then take place with all our resources in the room.

FELT SENSE IN ACTION

I am a guest in the house of two small girls and their parents. Nella is six and Bronnie is three. The girls are a lot of fun and we get on well. At dinner, I ask if they can help me with something. They say sure!

I ask them to choose two of their friends. They have no trouble, and they choose the same two girls (this is during Covid and their circle is not wide).

'Okay, choose just one of those two.'

'Iris!' they agree. Iris is their favourite friend at the moment.

'Yes, now think of Iris. And when you think of her, what happens in your body?'

Nella is the thoughtful one, you can see her checking it out. 'My heart goes all warm and soft.'

I smile. I have met little Iris, she is a sweet kid.

'How about you, Bronnie?'

Bronnie says she feels her heart soft too, but also 'tingly in my tummy'.

Then we go to the other friend – Amber.

Nella's answer is quick this time. 'My heart is thumpy, and I feel like I am jumping up and down inside.'

Bronnie's feeling is interesting. She is absolutely definite about it. It's in her *knees*; they feel wobbly.

The girls' mum gives me a covert smile. Amber is a bit 'full on', she explains.

Summing Up

If you take one thing from this whole book, let it be this: *it always starts with the body.*

We will soon show you how to use body signals to allow anxiety, grief, rage or fear to do their job and abate. And to let in the positive emotions – elation, contentment, gratitude, eroticism, tenderness, awe. All the good stuff! Feeling great is something your Wild Creature specialises in, and is a delightful help when you bring it back into your life.

We will also teach you the specific skill of how to follow or interrogate a body signal in order to learn something new about yourself, or those around you, or even solve problems in anything from house design to choosing a career, a spouse or a holiday. If you suffer from indecisiveness, this is a massive help.

Whatever you are addressing – today and every day – the first step is always noticing these signals and welcoming them as important. Soon, you will come to depend on them as a fantastic information source, an ally and friend.

As a takeaway core message, whenever you start to experience emotions that are not enjoyable or helpful, don't be swamped by them. Go looking for *where the sensations are*. Give them some room. Listen for what the story is that they are trying to tell you. Then you will begin to experience being your fullest self.

That is what we will learn in the chapters to come.

Chapter 4

The Man Who Found
Wild Creature Mind

The island of Skye lies in the Hebrides, the long chain of islands that lie off the west coast of Scotland, forming a bastion against the wild Atlantic swells. It's a beautiful place, but also a harsh one. And here, on a small country lane, underneath craggy peaks, a grey-bearded man is pushing against the wind, his hat shoved down hard to keep it in place.

His name is Dr Iain McGilchrist and he is no ordinary islander. Iain has been acclaimed by some commentators as one of the greatest thinkers of our times. Certainly, he has brought an unusual combination of knowledge and skills to his job of saving our mental health – if not civilisation itself.

McGilchrist has one of those minds that seems to range effortlessly across incredibly diverse fields of knowledge. He first came to note as a literary scholar at Oxford. Then he changed tack completely to study medicine, eventually making his way to psychiatry. He worked at the tough end of things, treating people who had serious brain impairments from accident or illness. He rose to be clinical director of the Maudsley Hospital in London, arguably the pinnacle of psychiatry in the UK. This in turn led him on to research in neuro-imaging, delving into the puzzles of schizophrenia and other disorders and how they arise from things going wrong in the brain. Judging from his two landmark (and very large) books, he seems to have read almost everything ever written about neuroscience, a field that has exploded in the last 30 years to include tens of thousands of researchers.

I remember reading the first few sentences of Iain's book, *The Master and His Emissary*. It wasn't a promising title, and the cover looked like a 1950s crime novel, so I almost ignored it when some friends pressed it on me. But my friends were very well-read folks whom I respected, so I made a start. Within minutes, I was hooked. Here was the clearest, most mind-blowing framing of what had gone wrong for my patients, and for the world, and a confirmation that there was deep science behind what we had been groping our way towards in the therapy field for the last 40 years.

McGilchrist argued – or *demonstrated* – that there was a reason we have a divided brain, and that healing depends on restoring the relationship between the two sides, and even more boldly, putting the better side in charge. Let me explain what this means.

Why Two Halves?

If you or I were designing a brain, we'd probably make it like a ball, nice and round. Then our thoughts wouldn't have to travel too far!

But that's not what nature did at all. As we saw in Chapter 2, our brain, and the brain of every living creature, has two halves. The two 'cortical hemispheres' are separate, only joined at the very bottom by a rubbery belt of neurons called the corpus callosum (which is Latin for 'tough bit'). If you studied psychology in the 20th century, you'd have likely been told that the corpus callosum sends messages from one side of the brain to the other. But brain scanning technology has found it's not quite that simple. Iain McGilchrist found that more than half of the neurons in the corpus callosum do not carry information, per se, they link instead to what are called 'inhibitor neurons'. They are, in effect, telling specific parts of the opposite hemisphere to shut up! *I've got this, just be quiet so I can concentrate!*

Astonishingly, less than two per cent of our brain cells on either side are connected to the opposite side in any direct way. From this reasoning, McGilchrist argues, there can only be one conclusion. That while our brain halves do communicate remarkably well, they are designed *to not do so* for significant moments in time.

So you have to ask the question: why? Why keep our mental faculties in two separate places like this? Why did nature give us a divided brain? To answer this, we need to go a bit wide. And to introduce you to a blackbird. So buckle in!

Science of Bits, and of Wholeness

Most of us who work in counselling and therapy get exasperated with research as it is done today. So much of it is frustratingly small stuff. And piecemeal. Like a shattered windscreen impossible to assemble into anything useful.

The reason lies in the way that academia works. The hardy souls who stay on to do postgraduate study are not set free to pursue whatever they wish! They are usually assigned a small area of study within the already narrow speciality of a person called their supervisor. This kind of makes sense, it means that a bigger project can be built on, little by little, in a team approach. The downside, though, is that research disappears into ever-shrinking rabbit holes of specialisation. (It's true even in medicine. A friend of mine was once told by a surgeon, 'I can't help with your feet, I'm a knee man!') Hardly anybody studies the big picture.

This is where meta minds are needed – people who independently go out and try to tie it all together. Interestingly, many of these have been women. Rachel Carson, author of the groundbreaking *Silent Spring*, was one such person. She basically founded the environment movement in the 1950s while still being prevented from holding a decent academic post. The American chemical industry mobilised massive forces against her, but she would not be scared off. We have her to thank for saving the land and ocean – and us – from the poison that was reaching every corner of the planet. Anthropologist Margaret Mead was another of these meta minds. And Virginia Satir, the creator of family therapy. Of course, some amazing men have also done this – most recently the two Davids, Graeber and Wengrow, with *The Dawn of Everything*, their stunning rewriting of our ideas about prehistory.

Iain McGilchrist (along with some other notables including the child development researcher Allan Schore) has done this for neuroscience. And his conclusions – which nobody is really disputing – are astounding. So, what is he saying? This is where the blackbird comes in.

Learning From a Bird

You have seen this with your own eyes, many times. It's early morning, and nobody is about yet. In the backyard of a suburban house, a blackbird flutters into sight, and perches on the fence. It scouts the lush lawn for any sign of worms. And sure enough, by some movement or sound – who knows how blackbirds do this? – it spies its breakfast. And then it does an odd thing. It tilts its head to look with its right eye and fixes the worm's location in its gaze. But it doesn't pounce yet. Now, it tilts its head the other way, so its left eye scans the garden, the sky, the back of the house. Then, and only then, it swoops down with unerring accuracy. In seconds, it has yanked the worm from the ground and shaken it down its throat.

As the final act, in a blur of wings, it is back on the fence again. Feeling, we can imagine, quietly pleased with itself.

So here is our first puzzle: what is this business with the left and right eye? And what has a story about a blackbird got to do with your mental health?

To make it through the day, every living creature – us included – has to do two very contradictory things inside its head. It has to be able to latch on to a goal and stay with it. For us, it might be getting breakfast, finishing off a project at work, or vigilantly guiding small children along a busy street. Single focus is very important. You can't daydream, for instance – at least, not too much – while riding a skateboard. Our brain, and the brain of pretty much every other creature on earth, has the ability to 'grasp' and 'hold' an idea or target, and hang in with it. To be 'single-minded'. Getting a degree, paying off a house, showing your ex that you are so much happier without them. Where would we be without focused goals? (Perhaps not the last one!)

But there is something more. For our little blackbird, having only a single focus could be a very dangerous thing. What if, intent on its worm breakfast, it did not take account of things that could spoil its plans? Like a cat, lurking in the bushes, itself very focused on its own goal: a blackbird that comes reliably to this lush lawn every morning at sunrise? What a gift! To *get* breakfast, and not *be* breakfast, has been the defining challenge of all living things from amoeba to stockbrokers. So every blackbird or any other creature, us included, through millions of years, has had to do two things simultaneously (or almost simultaneously). It has to – quite literally – keep an eye on the bigger picture. To scan its world for even the slightest hint of danger. I say 'scan' because danger is by definition not predictable. It could be anything, lurking in the bushes or in the sky above or coming down the highway. In a sense, it has to be the very *opposite* of focused; it has to be in a Zen-like openness to whatever comes. The defining quality of danger is that you just don't know where it's coming from, or what form it will take. You have to be 'wide open'.

While writing this, I talked to a very experienced soldier who said it is the same in a combat patrol. You 'go wide'. While certainly checking routinely – the ground in front, the points of cover ahead – there is also a kind of zoned-out feeling that senses for anything that might not add up, which your intuition picks up on and which cannot possibly be put into a checklist or manual. This ability, in her experience, saves countless lives.

So we have to be able to be focused, but also unfocused! A second of thought will make it clear that this creates a problem. No single mind can do both of these at the same time. The better you are at one, the worse you will be at the other. Each requires an entirely different approach, and in fact a different kind of information processing, and – drum roll here – *a whole different kind of brain.*

Nature had to solve this dilemma very early on – probably by the time of early fish. And so, from the very earliest time that brains evolved, they evolved in a very interesting way – *they split in two.*

Today, in every living creature, the cortical hemispheres each have what McGilchrist calls 'different ways of experiencing the world'. And so they are built very differently. They have totally different size and shape. They have different types of neurons, use a different mix of neurotransmitters, and are wired in a completely different way. (The left is compartmentalised, the right is much more of a whole.) This difference exists in all living creatures, but it is most apparent in humans. (As we evolved, our brains became *more* divided; this is not just some relic of our distant past.) It has to be in some way an advantage for survival.

The two sides bring different strengths. Every human activity that exists involves both sides of our brain, but their contribution is very different. After finding your Wild Creature and felt sense, you may find yourself aware of shifting from one side to another in almost everything you do. Put simply, we act, and evaluate, act and evaluate, even just walking around the house. It especially occurs when we are being creative; the artist makes a careful brush stroke, then he shifts hemispheres to see how he feels about it. And so it continues until the painting is finished.

Using Both Your Minds

Iain McGilchrist's book was released in 2010 to widespread acclaim in the scientific community and beyond. It summed up thousands of studies into how our brain and nervous system work and the existence of two minds across the divided hemispheres of the brain, including Iain's own work with brain-damaged patients. In people with severe brain injury, one of our minds can be enough to get by. But they are meant to work as a team, and for thousands of years in happier times for the human race, they did so perfectly well.

It was a tragic loss when, over recent centuries, as much as we made progress in the material and technical side of life, we lost the richness and helpfulness of our other side, and ended up so lost and unhappy. The right side of our brain is the part that helps enjoy life, because it connects with our body and all its senses. It also has richer connections to the 'primitive' limbic system, the emotional parts like the amygdala, and the memory banks of the hippocampus. So it receives all the information coming in from your senses and, like a hyperactive librarian, it cross-checks it all with memories already stored in your hippocampus. It especially searches for something that does not fit, or which might be relevant right now. (Once, while riding on beautiful King Island, my horse stopped stock-still on the trail because there was an aluminium can that had not been there a week before. That is the kind of memory intensity that your right brain possesses.)

One experience many people can relate to is that your right brain listens to every conversation within hearing range. For example, if you're at a crowded party and if someone mentions your name, it will let you know. This is what wakes the sleeping mother when her baby cries, even when no other noise penetrates her slumber. Your right hemisphere remembers books you have read and films you have seen. As you search through a book to find your place, it recognises which sentences you have already read.

You could never recall them in your left hemisphere, but your right knows: 'We've been here before!'

Your right brain is the part of you that is directly alive. Your left brain is a just a voyeur – only getting the second-hand reports, and not very accurate ones. Your Wild Creature Mind is the part that goes to the music festival of life, eats the delicious food and dances in the moonlight with the companion of your dreams! Your left hemisphere brain only gets to read about it in the news.

How to Hear Your Right Side

You will soon get to recognise which side is in charge, moment by moment in your life. As we go through our day, our chattery left side mind usually fills our thoughts, but flowing along inside us, our Wild Creature is making its own impressions, consulting our memories and shouting or whispering to us. And always, it will be through sensations in your body. You will soon recognise them telling you . . .

Look out!
Enjoy this.
Don't marry that person!
Your eight-year-old isn't telling the whole truth.
You're talking too much, stop and give the other person
    space.

Now is the time of the meeting to make a suggestion.

Get up and dance!

You've left your sunnies in the cafe.

That person's eyes are cold and don't match their smile.

Don't go down that alleyway.

You need to go for a walk.

Not the prawn salad!

Something in this relationship just broke.

Relax, everything is okay.

You are safe now.

It's okay to cry.

Can you see how varied and rich the help of Wild Creature Mind can be?

THREE MYTHS ABOUT THE BRAIN

Back in the 1970s there was a flurry of pop psychology about the two sides of the brain. Most of it, sadly, was wrong. The advent of brain scanning technology this century has given us a far more interesting and accurate picture. There have been three predominant myths about the hemispheres . . .

Myth 1: That the left side was rational, and the right side was emotional

IN FACT: the left side is *verbal*, yes, but that doesn't mean *rational*. Language can be used to reason, but words can also be used to deceive. The left side is easily swayed by things that 'sound' like they may sense – slogans and propaganda.

Iain McGilchrist notes that the left hemisphere, left on its own, is very prone to bias. Riddled with ego, it makes big errors of judgement, because it is so invested in being right. It oversimplifies, and is not designed for ambiguity or nuance, which the right hemisphere excels at.

In fact, the left side is *more* emotional. It is especially prone to *anger*, as it just hates being shown to be wrong. The left hemisphere is the reason for the well documented finding that 'people who know the least, think they know the most'.

The left side thinks by taking things apart, and treats things (including people) as objects. It doesn't deal with the fact that other people have feelings, have their own point of view or even matter. It sees a tree as firewood, an animal as food, and a woman as . . . well, you get the idea. The right side is open to complexity and can manage contradictions or tensions between two valid points of view. And life is full of those.

Some cultures – like traditional Eastern cultures – are much more right brained. As a child, I was always flummoxed by those English proverbs which seemed to contradict – 'fools rush in where angels fear to tread' or 'he who hesitates is lost'. Which one was right?

Asian proverbs tend to embrace the nuances of the real world. McGilchrist cites the Chinese saying 'too much humble is halfway proud'. Can you see what is being done there? It's not a prescriptive answer, but points to a sensitivity: you can take something too far, and for the wrong reasons. Be alert to your own motivation and be reserved in all things. It's beautifully Taoist.

Myth 2: The idea that the left brain is masculine, and the right brain feminine

IN FACT: this gets into another myth – of women being more emotional and men more rational. Whereas most people would now say that's the other way around. Women in our culture express emotions more easily so they *seem* more emotional, but this leads to them being less pent up and driven by those emotions. It's possible that women are more in touch with their right hemisphere. Better at seeing the big picture, being empathic, reading social cues.

Possibly men need more help to access their right hemisphere (and stand to benefit most from the ideas in this book). McGilchrist points to research showing that many of the difficulties of neurodiverse people, and people with schizophrenia, also arise through difficulty accessing their right hemisphere. Certainly for me (male, neurodivergent, English) Wild Creature methods have proven a life-changing source of help, contributing to my huge enthusiasm to get them out there.

Myth 3: The right hemisphere is the creative part of us
IN FACT: creativity is best when *both* sides are really steaming along collaboratively. For example, a creative person might create a tune or begin an artwork with their left hemisphere, and then check with their right hemisphere's felt sense to tell them, yes, that's beautiful. It's as if the right hemisphere knows what we are aiming for, and lets us know when we are getting close. The interplay of left and right is going on at high speed continually in the creative process. In fact, there is no human process or activity that does not involve both sides.

These are the myths of the right hemisphere. But what then is the truth of it?

The truth is a very radical one, which Iain McGilchrist argues over thousands of pages in his two monumental tomes. That our right hemisphere is where we are supposed to 'live', where we should centre our being. When we live in our right hemisphere, we are receptive to both what is around us and what is happening inside us in response. This helps us inhabit a larger self, inseparable from the living world around us.

When we are open to the sensory world, our life just works so much better. We are present, and we are aware. We are empathic and connected to everyone we meet. We use our left hemisphere in the way it was intended – for analysis, reasoning and communication of specifics. But we never get trapped and mistaken left-hemisphere thinking for absolute reality.

Wild Creature Mind – the extraordinary biological system of the right hemisphere and the entire body's sensing and acting – is the real 'us'. We can walk out of that cramped and lonely place of 20th-century left-hemisphere thought, and be fully human. And it's not even all that hard.

Neither I nor Iain McGilchrist would want to be denigrating the value of our left brain. Its ability to explain and to analyse is one of the most powerful things about being human. It can bring order and sense to life, and we spend years teaching our children to 'think things through', 'use words', and 'consider the views of others'. But we have to be watchful of its failings. If we help bring Wild Creature awareness alongside left-brain thinking, then we really bring forth a superb human being.

There is one more thing that is really important. In the second half of his book, McGilchrist takes things a big step further. He looks at how our whole culture lost its right-brain Wild Creature faculties. We became so trapped in the left hemisphere that we let the right fall silent not just in our own heads, but in the way we organise the world. (This process took place over several thousand years, it was no small thing.) McGilchrist is convinced that this is the real reason for our terrible problems today with mental health, and with planetary health. We can grasp – at possessions, people or experiences – but we can't *enjoy*, so we are never satisfied. We aren't at home in our own skin, or the sensory world around us. We are jarring in our interactions. We can dismantle things, but not put them back together (either our marriages, or the planetary ecosystem). Not to mince words, we have become stupid. As is to be expected with only half a brain.

Who We Put in Charge

There is one more lesson from the blackbird, perhaps the most important of all.

The hungry bird pauses on the fence, and its left brain is going crazy, ready to pounce. It's basically going, 'Worm, worm, worm! Let's go, let's get it, it's just right there, quick, before it's gone!' like a kid in a toyshop. And its right brain is going, 'Well, let's just hang on a minute. No pouncing until we check that it's safe. My mother disappeared on this lawn, there was nothing left but feathers!'

And only when the right brain has done its scan does it give the go-ahead to the impatient left. So, in our actual Wild Creature, this is how the two hemispheres cooperate. And my question to you, dear reader, is this: who is the boss?

Clearly, the right hemisphere is calling the shots. And that is how all animals function – wide focus, big picture, consult your memory banks and listen to your gut. In a properly functioning brain, or society, the left hemisphere is merely the servant. Our right hemisphere evaluates the whole context, the many dimensions that come into play. Only then does it 'recruit' the left hemisphere to work out a plan of action. For example, a father might have a vague but strong feeling that something is wrong with one of their children (or their spouse). So he waits until bedtime when it will be peaceful enough to have a quiet talk. He has a gut feeling, but is thoughtful about how to implement it.

Wild Creature Mind has a calmer, more nuanced approach. It isn't binary, it can take in ten different points of view and feel its way forward. As you begin to change, you will find that grabbing and grasping – the methods of the left brain – are happening less and less. Your field of view widens and grows so that you move gently, with a sense of full awareness, reading the signs as you go. It's a beautiful place to be, and when you use it, you will start to become the calm one in your family or team who helps everyone to not panic, and get things right. And it just feels a whole lot better to live this way.

EXERCISE: HOW YOUR RIGHT BRAIN GETS THE JOKE

Want to catch your Wild Creature Mind in action? Try listening to a comedian, or just a single joke. In an instant too fast for thought, you 'get' the joke and laugh. Then, a split-second later, you 'understand' why it is funny. But the explanation of a joke is never funny – the left hemisphere is not where the fun is had!

It's the 'shock' of a joke that makes it so exhilarating and pleasurable. Each joke builds tension then relieves it, which is why comedians traditionally go into edgy places. Edgy is a real skill because over the edge isn't funny, so you have to feel your way with this as well.

Here is one to try.

A woman catches a taxi in a big city to travel to a distant suburb. The journey proceeds in silence. After about ten minutes, she remembers another errand she needs to do on the way, so she reaches forwards and taps the driver on the shoulder.

He utters a bloodcurdling scream, hits the brakes, skids and swerves through a fence into a park, crosses the lawn and ends in a duck pond.

Recovering her composure, she apologises. 'I'm SO sorry. I didn't mean to startle you.'

He says, 'No, it's not your fault. It's my first day driving taxis. Before that, for 25 years, I drove a hearse.'

(Hope you liked that. And hope you notice that you 'got it' before you worked it out.)

Summing Up

There has been a paradigm shift in neuroscience, which is quite without precedent. It is the realisation that we have not just two separate brains in our head, but two actual minds. The right hemisphere is a neglected supercomputer of extraordinary help and ability, more realistic and more connected than our lonely little thinking mind on the left. Our right hemisphere, via our body, is a portal to our natural wholeness as an organism, and to living with sensitivity to the lives around us.

McGilchrist leads the charge on this, but the whole field of brain study is in the vanguard (Allan Schore, Dan Siegel, Leslie Ellis, and many others who we will meet in these pages are in strong accord).

When I picture Iain at work, he is like Gandalf poring over scrolls to find a secret that the whole future of the world pivots on. We are in one mighty mess, through our left-brained way of blundering through life, disconnected and selfish, technocratic and machine-like. The universe is a song, not a coal mine. We can rejoin the choir. Mental health and species health are one and the same. And it's not even all that hard.

Chapter 5

There is Something in Me . . .

James is lying in bed. It's 3 am and he is in the spare bedroom, unable to sleep.

James is a paramedic, aged 36, a husband and a dad. His partner has their sick toddler with her in their main bed tonight. James has worries about his work, about their finances and of course – tonight – about whether their child is okay. He desperately needs some rest.

Rather than toss and turn as he would have in the past, James uses something that has been taught to him by a counsellor he has been seeing for a couple of weeks.

First, instead of fighting against or trying to tough the problem out, or just thinking round and round in circles, he does something different. He sends his attention down into his body and searches for *where the bad feeling seems to be located*. At this stage, James is only aware that he feels stressed; it's not differentiated in any way at all. Fairly quickly, though, he can feel that it's mostly around his chest, and somewhat towards the front of his body.

He then uses a slightly unusual form of words that his therapist has taught him to say to himself (out loud or silently, whatever works). By saying this sentence – even a bit sheepishly at first – he is attempting something new, in the hope of finding escape from a very desperate condition he has not been able to defeat. This isn't a panacea, but it is like the opening of a small chink of light which might possibly begin his journey to health. The sentence is one you are going to find yourself becoming very familiar with.

There alone, in his tangled and sweaty bed, he murmurs to himself, 'There is something in me . . .'

James does not finish the sentence yet; its purpose is to start a process – to recognise something objectively true, which is that there is a vague, undefined cluster of sensations at the heart of his unease. And crucially, that another part of him can *observe* that, from a distance. It's like his head looking down at his body.

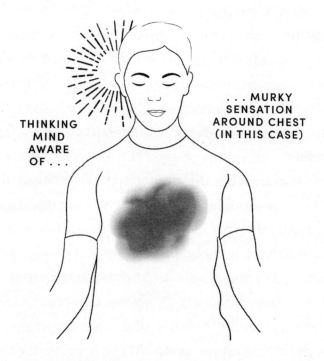

THINKING
MIND
AWARE
OF . . .

. . . MURKY
SENSATION
AROUND CHEST
(IN THIS CASE)

'There is something in me' is a form of words that is a little bit old-fashioned. Characters in Jane Austen novels say things like, 'There is something in me that longs for the sea,' or 'There is something in me that wants to give him a good smack in the mouth.' (Okay, maybe not Jane Austen for that one.) In the days before television and the internet, people used to speak with more precision. 'There is something in me' implicitly acknowledges that this impulse or yearning is not the totality of us, *but it is there*. It recognises that we have competing urges, and that's okay. 'I won't run away to the South Seas, but part of me definitely would like to.'

We all have many parts, as you will know from every time you have experienced a conflict within yourself. (A large box of chocolates in your fridge can be all it takes!) Two sides of us emerge around every major or minor decision we face, but that's not all there is. In fact, there is a whole bunch of odd characters in most of us, bickering and taking sides, sabotaging and upstaging each other. But for now, the key thing to know is that often, a part of us – especially a very emotional one – can take us over. We get swamped by it, and think, *This is who I am. This desperation, this anxiety, this rage, this heartache, is all I am.* And that can be a despairing feeling. But the answer is a surprisingly simple mental 'hack'. We begin by noticing that this upset state is at heart, a *physical sensation*. And we begin that by simply observing 'There is something in me . . .' and noticing where the feeling is located. (On page 98 we have more help with how to do this.) We give it some compassionate attention.

We do this because this discomfort or agitation is not some enemy or innate weakness – our bodies are much better designed than that. It is a part of us that is seeking to get our attention – shouting in fact. And by delineating and attending to the physical felt sense that is present, we can begin to integrate our own inner world, and find peace – however tough our circumstances. Then Wild Creature Mind, the driving force underneath all our upsets, can be allowed to do its healing work. This is a big thing to grasp all at once, but we'll follow James over several chapters as his story shows how it is done.

How 'Something in Me' Creates Mental Freedom

'There is something in me . . .' is such a simple sentence, but its effect in the brain is remarkable. At the moment of using these words to describe his experience (noticing that he has this inner event going on in his body), James's awareness has automatically split into two parts. One is the location of the distress, which may be tense, roiling or any number of unpleasant things, while the other is the objective observer, a place of stillness and quiet friendliness, standing aside and just . . . noticing. And this brings the beginning of a sense that, however intense the suffering – including strong physical pain of injury or illness – *it is not all of you*. It's not all-encompassing, all-defining. It has a location and it has a nature that can be described. *It doesn't hurt everywhere.* (Friends who have strong chronic pain have told me that they use this to survive the worst bouts – they locate a place inside them that feels okay, more pain-free, and they work to locate themselves in that place.)

James is aware that the discomfort he feels is located in the upper half of his body, around the front of his chest, his heart – which is beating quite fast – and up around his shoulders. He can sense it as a zone with some key locations within it that are more acutely affected. It's pretty strong and distressing, but to notice its location somehow helps. It's like it has a life of its own (it does, as we shall soon learn). This part of him is taking a particular form at this moment; he can almost picture it, like a dark shadow with blurred edges.

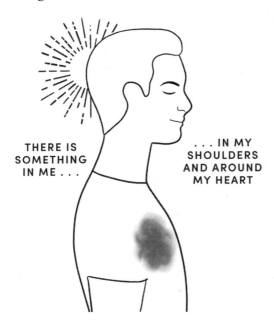

THERE IS
SOMETHING
IN ME . . .

. . . IN MY
SHOULDERS
AND AROUND
MY HEART

As James lies there, even this simple 'thought action' brings a tiny change in the sensation itself. He doesn't want to get his hopes up, but something is starting to change. The felt sense inside him shifts, just a little, perhaps shrinking, perhaps diffusing or even changing into a different configuration.

In taking these small steps, James is experiencing that he has a part of him – a wild and unruly part – which is trying to tell him something. If he takes a better attitude to it then, like any living thing, it responds to that. Your positivity or negativity towards your Wild Creature will make all the difference in the world, because we are not meant to be at odds with ourselves. (That's what the Mary Oliver line in the epigraph of this book is saying.) Because James is welcoming his Wild Creature signals, it is becoming less desperate to get through to him, more willing to stop yelling at him.

James proceeds as his counsellor taught him. As he begins to actually locate the 'quality' of the sensations, he now completes the sentence. He knows that it is always murky and vague to begin with; that is the nature of felt sense. It is new, and takes some exploring to emerge. 'Something in me feels . . . uh, bad, stirred up, kind of tight.' It is fine to be vague, to try out different guesses. This is what a respectful relationship is like – we humbly enquire, while being willing to be wrong. The Wild Creature part of us notices that we are giving it our best shot, that we are open, not hectoring or impatient. That we are creating a space for something to happen.

As James fleshes out what the sensations are, and where they live, he is progressively less 'caught' in the worries. Instead, it is becoming clearer that this is a physical sensation, and it has an actual delineated region where it is taking place. His amygdala, deep in his brain, starts to calm. His breathing, quite out of awareness, is starting to slow down.

He continues to keep his attention in his body, inside himself, noticing little twitches and shifts. It's so slight, he wonders if he's just imagining it. But no, the sensations are becoming more distinct. Like a shy animal, emerging from the undergrowth, it comes from the shadows and allows itself to be seen. James's role is to be quiet and attentive, and to feel for the signs of its emergence. He does this by narrowing down exactly where this 'wrongness' lives, where in his body he knows he is not feeling right.

And suddenly, he is aware that there is something new.

There is a tension down the front of his body, most noticeable as a pressure around his heart, but also in a kind of tunnel down to his stomach, where another node of clenchedness is clearly present.

If he had drawn the felt sense, it might have looked like this:

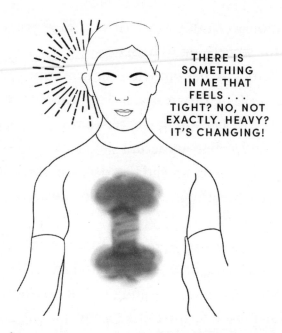

THERE IS SOMETHING IN ME THAT FEELS... TIGHT? NO, NOT EXACTLY. HEAVY? IT'S CHANGING!

The quality of James's upset felt sense might be static, or it might be moving – swirling or changing, pulsating or even altering in location. He stays with this for a few moments, just seeing what happens. It's still quite uncomfortable, but he is encouraged by his engagement, by the fact he is doing something proactive.

Making it Welcome

As he begins to relax, James now remembers an important step his therapist showed him, and in fact used with him in their most recent session. He had overlooked this; next time he will do it earlier in the sequence. (It's hard to be organised in your thoughts at 3 am!) He deliberately thinks a greeting to the set of sensations in his body. He acknowledges them, in the same way you might say hello to your dog or cat when you return home. He says or thinks, 'I see you.' And then a bigger, more intentional act of thought – 'You are welcome.' He feels slightly foolish doing this step, but it also makes him feel oddly emotional. This has added a new quality to the objective observer part of him that has sprung up; one part of him is now making friends with another part. And it's a friendship that is really important for his mental health.

The sensations in James's body seem to be affected, just subtly, by this attitudinal shift. They start to lose their tightness, and as they do that, they increase in size, into his chest. In doing so, they begin to fade away.

His stomach gurgles a little.

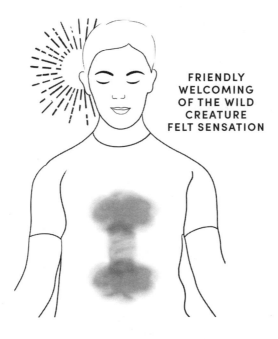

FRIENDLY WELCOMING OF THE WILD CREATURE FELT SENSATION

How Does it Work?

There may be a part of you wondering, how does this all work? Why does our body have these felt-sense storms going on inside, and why does it work to welcome them and give them room to be there?

The answer is quite simple: we are fixing a relationship with ourselves that has been broken for a very long time. We are restoring a natural process. The wild part inside most people today is unhappy and neglected because in our childhoods, it was either driven into hiding, or at very best, was just not mentioned.

When James was a child, his parents were under lots of stress. Paying bills, keeping your job, finding affordable housing – these can all make it hard to find time to be loving and kind. They were good and responsible parents, but they did not have much time for James's inner world, or talking to him about it. They easily defaulted to harsh words. So naturally, in order to avoid making things worse, little James began to take the same approach to himself. He split in two – a tender, vulnerable part lived on inside him and the other part beat up on himself for being so. It's rather shocking to realise that often the most abusive relationship in our lives is the one we have with ourselves.

So when James says, 'Hello, I see you,' and, even more importantly, 'Welcome,' to his own felt sense, that is a big change in how he is running the dynamics of his own mind.

The relationship between his two parts is tentatively stepping onto a new trajectory. It's like marriage counselling for the relationship inside him.

The therapist he is seeing is a living example of this attitude. She is kind, unhurried, but also very concerned for him that he gets to a better place. As a paramedic, James deserves the same good care he has given to other people in distress. (Everyone deserves this. We are all little, wild creatures on the inside, and this is simply what is natural and right to meet our basic needs. Care and attention are needed in all growing humans, at whatever age.)

James, still lying in his disarrayed bed, finally breathing more slowly and evenly, takes a last step. He sends some thoughts to this other part along these lines: *Thank you for being here. I want you here. I know you have something to say to me.* And with this thought, there comes a stronger change in the muscles and nerve endings that have been tensed and clenched around the felt sense part, trying to squash or contain it. As he notices that, they change some more. Perhaps they move up from his heart to his throat, or they soften and simply go away. Or they turn into some surge of emotion which flows through and out of him. They are physical phenomena and have physical ways to resolve. They might simply turn into a big, single shudder through his body, or to a sudden pricking of tears or, simplest of all, an enormous sigh. He might move about in some spontaneous way.

A seemingly intractable tension that he had been trying without success to resolve through endless tangled thought has been handed off to the part of his being which actually can deal with such things. Whatever happens, the result is the same: happy, relieved and no longer at war with himself, James and his Wild Creature Mind fall asleep.

But this is not just catharsis. Something in his left hemisphere has changed as well. Little by little, some new meaning is emerging. Tomorrow and in the days to come, James will have new thoughts, insights and ways to set his priorities. Both sides of him have begun to find some trust, and that is always powerful. More fragile and difficult messages might now begin to be allowed to emerge.

A start has been made. We will soon meet James's counsellor as she takes this tiny beginning and helps James get to the bottom of what will be a major turning point in his career and his life.

And we have hopefully got you, dear reader, started in understanding that you don't have to fight against anxiety, stress, even post-traumatic stress and pain conditions. In fact, the complete opposite is the case.

You have begun to sense what is possible with your Wild Creature Mind.

Summing Up

What we in the modern world call 'anxiety' – and try to suppress or medicate to make go away – is not a malfunction. It is part of our mind trying to get our attention, to confront something or work it through. The start of this has to involve getting to the source. Our Wild Creature is thrashing about, saying, 'Listen to me.'

The technique of acknowledging 'there is something in me' sweeps us from being overwhelmed to discovering that this is just a part of our own mind, wanting to communicate.

If we go towards it gently, make it welcome, show it that we want to know its point of view, then there is an immediate settling inside us. We haven't yet got the message, but we are ready to hear it.

We are ready to take the next big step – to healing. Or to action. Your body will tell you which.

DEEPER DIVE: WELCOME? YOU HAVE TO BE JOKING!

It is a big thing to send welcoming thoughts to a part of you that is painful, that you would give anything to be rid of. People drink, take drugs, hurt other people, even take their own lives, because of mental pain. (We call it mental pain, but in fact it is always in our bodies that we feel it.) A person who takes their own life (and I have worked with many people who have *almost* done so) does not do so because they want to be dead. *They just want to stop hurting*. And the way to stop hurting, incredibly, is to stop fighting the sensations and *let them move through us*.

This is the very opposite of what we feel like doing, and a reason why you may need a person to support you in doing so. Boiled down to its very essence, therapy works because someone else makes it safe for us to give ourselves over to the pain we carry inside. To 'let go'. It can be as simple as crying when we haven't been able to. But it might be to feel absolute fury when in the past all we could do was cry. Children often need their parents' help to 'process' emotions, to have them shake and shudder and weep and be spoken out loud, and we adults are no different. Eventually, we learn to do this for ourselves, but we will never not need others to feel really right in the world. We are a communal species like an elephant or a lion, not like a lone wombat in a burrow. And we heal best together.

The genius of Wild Creature Mind is that by taking on distress as purely sensation, we find that the emotional impact is lessened. For example, loneliness, though it can be the worst feeling in the world, is actually a specific set of sensations (often in one's skin and heart, or a hollowness going right through your middle, though each person feels it uniquely). The key to surviving with being away from loved ones is to realise that loneliness, awful as it is, is a sensation. You can even counter it somewhat: imagine being held and safe. As you do this, you should be able to feel the hormones release, oxytocin and serotonin flooding back into your bloodstream. It's the same for any painful emotion – take shame, for example. You've let down someone you care about, or worse caused them some harm. Your body burns all over, you feel yourself cringing away inside. (It's worse if you were shamed or hit as a child.) But what you must do is 'stand with' these sensations, and not run from them. They convey to the person you've hurt, that you genuinely are ashamed. It's painful, but it doesn't kill you. It is a sign of caring, and of taking responsibility. And those are admirable traits.

Our Wild Creature helps us to let go of mental pain by reminding us that it is actually just physical pain. And it is carrying us to a new place, if we can stay with it and let it do its job. My observation of people in terrible grief, for example, is that when we finally begin to sob and keen with distress, there are always thoughts that come to the fore and are actually spoken amid the tears. Our left hemisphere is taken to new places by the communication with the right. Core misbeliefs are cracked open. 'I couldn't take away her pain,' or 'If only I had not let him drive that night.' These thoughts are pivotal because as our mind surfaces them, they move along like leaves on a flooding river, swept from sight. As agonising as they are, a part of us knows these thoughts are of no use. And we begin to soften our hearts.

Grief is all about the body. But so is all mental pain. Our job is not to ignore it, but to actually use those sensations to carry us inwards. We might feel great solid lumps in our throat, chest or gut. We have to make room for them, soften to them, let them swell up and wash over us.

If we can show tenderness towards that part of us, literally seeing it as a small lonely or frightened creature that needs our care and attention, then we can self-nurture and find a way forward.

If we are not able to do this by ourselves, then it's important to seek help and allow someone else to care for us while we relearn to be safe and welcome in the world.

GETTING HELP

Unaddressed mental pain is harmful, it can turn into either self-mistreatment or violence against others, and so I strongly recommend getting help if you find the methods in this book are not enough. (Do finish reading it first, we have barely begun!) Luckily it has become much more acceptable and normal to seek counselling when we get stuck at some time in our life. In Australia the best way to find psychological help is to go to your family doctor and ask for a 'mental health plan'. This gives you a number of subsidised sessions (currently up to ten) with a psychologist or counsellor, if your GP thinks that you would benefit.

The GP may suggest the therapist, but you may want to ask around locally to find a good one recommended by word of mouth. And even then, I recommend that you 'audition' your therapist with a single first session, and you will sense whether they are right for you. Generally, I find that having someone older than you is best. And for women, a same-sex counsellor is ideal. For men, it is not so crucial, but for serious stress problems, a woman may be best, and for difficulties with marriage and adult life, an older male can fill a fathering or mentoring gap as they will better understand the male condition. In times of urgent need or distress though, do access the phone and online help avenues listed below, until you can see someone face to face. You can also use these if you just aren't ready to see a therapist, but can handle phone or online contact more anonymously.

Lifeline on 13 11 14

Kids Helpline on 1800 551 800

MensLine Australia on 1300 789 978

Suicide Call Back Service on 1300 659 467

Beyond Blue on 1300 22 46 36

Headspace on 1800 650 890, which is for young people aged 12–25

Remember, above all, these two things. You are valuable, and you deserve help. And with that help, you will one day be well, and can help make the world better for others in pain. So we can all one day dance in the sunshine and be happy and free.

Chapter 6

A Tiger in the Forest: How Our Bodies Talk to Us

We've been introduced now to the very radical idea of having two minds. Alongside our familiar, chattery mind we have our second – Wild Creature – mind, keeping watch over our lives, and always ready to alert or guide us. So the billion-dollar question becomes: 'how can we talk to it?' How do we get to know this super-sensitive and all-remembering part of ourselves? And ask for its advice?

To begin to understand, we have to ask another question: how did all creatures throughout aeons of time hear what their mind was telling them? To answer that, let's go back to the wild.

A tiger moves silently and carefully through the forest. It's been tracking a large deer for many hours and now, late in the day, it has found it, grazing peacefully in a sun-dappled clearing. The tiger has expended a lot of energy and time on this hunt, so it is intensely focused. It treads with infinite care to get close enough to leap. But suddenly, something happens: the birds that have been noisily calling all day go silent. And in that second, the tiger freezes, its enormous paw hovering midair.

Now, tigers do not have words. It does not think, 'Hmm, the birds just went silent!' or 'That doesn't feel right' or even 'Maybe I had better wait to see what's wrong.' Its senses, honed over millions of years of cat family evolution, simply tell it, 'Stop.' It's automatic. It's a felt sense to freeze, and felt sense is incredibly effective at preserving and sustaining life.

Your Wild Creature Mind works directly from senses to right hemisphere to action. It is lightning fast. It isn't that the tiger needs to notice its felt sense and *decide* to hover its paw silently in midstep. *Felt sense stops the paw.* Just like that.

In my book *Fully Human*, I told the story of a young mother Andie who listened to her felt sense, her Wild Creature Mind, and by acting faster than thought would have allowed, narrowly escaped an attacker in a suburban car park. Her gut feeling sent her into a panic, which made no sense to her at all, and she fled the scene, all the time thinking, 'What is wrong with me?' Subsequent events proved that this probably saved her life.

We've all experienced these moments of 'alarm signals going off'. My wife Shaaron once pulled our family up as we walked down an extremely crowded city street in South East Asia at night and said, 'This doesn't feel right.' It was something about the crowd, but we didn't stay to analyse; we awkwardly made our way against the streaming crowds. Minutes later, a riot broke out between locals and visiting servicemen. It involved hundreds of people and covered several city blocks. Shaaron's senses perceived *something* in the mood of the crowd which she could not put into words.

I have never been in a group of people anywhere where people did not have stories of having a 'gut sense' that saved them in some way, large or small. Or who had avoided a bad decision just because something inside them had warned them. (Or chose badly while knowing deep down it would lead to disaster – we don't always listen to our Wild Creature Mind!)

Like a thousand generations of tigers, these signals are 'felt'. They are sensory, coming from inside our bodies. Even the most dried-up intellectual person implicitly acknowledges this: 'I'm not *comfortable* with what you are saying.'

Now, a part of you is going to be wondering how is it that we have to listen to *our bodies* to get these messages from our right brain? Couldn't our two minds just *talk* to each other? Or send pictures or something? The answer is that Wild Creature Mind is actually sending signals to the body anyway! In an animal, this is all it needs to do. The bird flies, the whale dives, the lioness lowers herself into the long grass to stay out of sight. Sensation drives action, and everything just flows. The signals are extremely refined and intricate when they need to be – think of those beautiful flocks of thousands of starlings that make us gasp with their aerial ballet in the cool evenings of autumn. Those birds are not thinking, *Go left now, watch out, now swoop down!* They feel it in the way a superb musician or dancer does. They abandon themselves to their right hemisphere.

In fact animals are so responsive to what is around them, that they are essentially merged with it, and need no identity at all. (Few animals even have a formed sense of 'self'; that is something which exists only in the higher mammals. A chimp can recognise itself in a mirror, a cow wouldn't have the first idea! The small birds in my garden attack their reflections in the window!)

How We Can Listen

The whole premise of this book comes back to this: every mental faculty a wild creature has, we have too. We did not lose capacities in the long journey to being human. Your Wild Creature Mind is right there, waking and sleeping and you can become attuned to it as completely as one of those starlings! You can tune in to it while walking to work, waiting in a queue, lying in the arms of your loved one.

To make it easier at first, it's good to take a few preparatory steps.

Breathe a big, soft breath or two. Soften your eyes a little. Then, go down the middle of your body and notice what is happening. Any sensation at all. Even if you feel nothing – well, nothing is a sensation too.

Rather like those old polaroid photos that start out blurry and grey, something will begin to clarify a little. You can locate where it is first of all, and then its shape and its qualities. You may not have time to go further, but just doing this will start things happening. Every little bit makes you more integrated, and safer.

For instance, right now, as you are reading this book, it's happening. Your body is giving little signs of assent, annoyance or disagreement, just below your level of awareness. You are reading the words, but your Wild Creature is looking over your shoulder, going, 'Yep' or 'Nup'. (Some readers may be reminded of Calvin's toy tiger in the *Calvin and Hobbes* cartoons. Or even more vividly, the personal daemon creatures in Philip Pullman's *His Dark Materials* novels. The magical animals that manifest alongside Philip's characters are a stunning parallel of how our brain actually works.)

Your Wild Creature reads the world around you. It is first and foremost an early warning system. If something is amiss, it rings alarm bells. In fact, it can become quite agitated if it senses that you are going the wrong way, or not addressing something which needs attention. But because it has no words, its channel of communication can only be through your body. Its signals go down the nerves to your stomach, heart, gut, skin, muscles, throat and face, and it speaks to you through direct, complex and very sensitive physical sensations. What Eugene Gendlin called the 'felt sense'.

Felt sense is what happens when you have a qualm or a misgiving. Whether we notice this or not, it is always a physical sensation first. It's an odd idea for us to realise that little twinges in our stomach or heart or throat can be complex messages coming from our right cerebral cortex, but it's always been quietly there in our language – we have names for it like 'gut feelings' and 'hunches'.

Remember Einstein talking about a 'visceral' feeling that told him where to search in solving relativity? It is that sophisticated. But even in everyday life, our language is full of this awareness: 'my heart sank' or 'I was gutted'. We know some people are 'creepy' because we feel it in our skin. It crawls. These are ancient, perceptive whisperings that kept our ancestors alive, and were passed down to us for the same purpose. In an animal, as we've said, it actually organises behaviour, helps make it harmonious and graceful.

Felt sense is a force beyond thought which nonetheless shapes the living world. It stops the lion in its tracks and lifts the shore bird into the air. It brings the great flocks of grazing beasts on the Serengeti into migration. It draws the teenager out of their parents' house on a warm summer evening and into a larger world.

As you get more used to it, in touch with it, felt sense can guide all your interactions, and all your daily activities. In a fully functioning person, left-brain thinking alternates with right-brain awareness from second to second, so your decision-making and movement through your day is more alert and responsive; more *harmonised*. You get along with people because you are 'reading' them with your right-brain faculties, and gauging how to treat them sensitively. You already have experienced this – sometimes you just feel a sense of flowing pleasure and grace in your day; at other times, nothing quite works, it's one stuff-up piling on another. And you can feel it in other people too; sometimes a person just feels really comfortable to be around, or admirable and congruent. And sometimes, you meet people who feel very, very wrong.

Don't worry if you find tracking your felt sense to be a hit-and-miss affair at first. It's likely that your Wild Creature is not sure yet if it wants to trust you. As you show respect towards it, it emerges from the thickets of your mind and, little by little, becomes a friendly companion. And like any good companion, it both comforts you and enlivens your world.

MAKING A HOME FOR JOY . . .

Remember when you were falling in love? There was someone you were really drawn to, and it felt like they might be drawn to you too? It was on many levels – warmth, liking, erotic charge, intellectual challenge all mixed in together. Electricity was in the air. Even the uncertainty of whether you imagined it or not, added to the intensity. And then, by some mix of accident and contrivance, they touched you or you touched them. Maybe they brushed against you as you got out of a car? And suddenly time stopped, and from that couple of moments of skin on skin, electricity spread all through your body, every nerve ending coming alive. You remember, don't you? It was burned into your soul.

Pleasure and feeling-just-rightness is the domain of our Wild Creature side. (Stroke a cat or dog and see how they lean into the pleasure of it with their whole body.) Whenever we have nice things going on around us – music, scenery, laughter, good food, a summer's day – we can do two things. We can pass it over, and zip back into our left hemisphere and plan our schedule. Or we can let it in. Appreciation and allowing of deep pleasure is a decision; we go into our body, notice what is happening, and then we give it more space. It's a kind of attention, that softens the edges of the place where the pleasure originates, as if we are letting down the dam for the flooding to take place.

As fully as we can, we stay in Wild Creature body sensation mode, and allow the happiness to ripple into our darkest corners and wash them clean. Happiness in this life is fleeting. Do not let it go to waste. Let it nourish and energise you so you can continue the journey with a spring in your step.

Locating and Describing Your Felt Sense to Get Both Minds Talking

Tuning in to your felt sense starts with locating it. When you want to make progress with a problem, or are feeling bad and want to get unstuck, then start to notice where the felt sense is happening. Always use the phrase or be aware that 'there is something in me . . .' then move to locate where it is.

1. Is it high or low in your torso, in your throat, or even occasionally up higher, in and around your head, or even in your legs?

2. Is it more to the front of your body, or the back, or just in the middle? For example, it could be a shield-like hardness at the front of your chest, or almost shrinking back inside you.

3. Does it have a shape? For example, is it cylindrical or spherical, with hard edges, or cloudy and undefined? It can be diagonal, or more to the left or the right. It doesn't usually correspond to organs or anything anatomical, though it might if you rushed breakfast, haha.

4. Very often, your heart will be involved, and so if you don't notice much at all, be aware of the sensations around your heart region, which you might just be so accustomed to you don't notice.

5. Once you've located it (and it might move or change when you pay attention to it), you can try out words that describe the quality or nature of it. Here are some typical words people often use, though you will find your own – there are hundreds of words that might fit.

- aching
- a falling away
- clenching
- empty, or a big empty hole
- fluttering
- grabbing hands
- heart goes warm and soft
- heat or glow
- holding on
- jumping up and down inside
- legs wanting to run
- locked up
- movements or swirls
- numbing
- pulsations, like an exaggerated heartbeat
- shadowy and faint
- sinking
- stirring
- thumping
- tightening
- tingly
- twinge
- warming
- wobbly

It is built in to the process that your first guesses are never quite right, because the felt sense only emerges as a result of your efforts. You aren't so much 'labelling' it as 'interacting with' it, and it will reveal itself more.

Your animal mind will give you a sense of 'Yes' or 'No' to the words you choose. By building this connection, automatically your two hemispheres will start to synchronise a little more. You will start to feel either more comfortable, or more resolute and integrated. You may also have flashes of understanding, small or large, broadening your insight and perspective. Be open to being changed and enlarged by both sides of your brain getting in sync.

When Wild Creature Mind is Wrong

There's an important thing to say here, lest we get the wrong idea. Wild Creature Mind is amazing, yes, but that doesn't mean it is *infallible*.

If you think of your own life, quite often you will have anxiety just happen out of the blue, or unhappy memories or thoughts will rise up and spoil your day.

Surely this is coming from your Wild Creature Mind – since you are not 'choosing' to have these upsetting thoughts? Well, it's complicated – let's explain . . .

It's normal and within the nature of our Wild Creature Mind to respond wholeheartedly to whatever happens – to cry, shake, weep, get hugs, run, shout, dance – and to not store any leftover emotions. Creatures in the wild experience terrifying near misses – think of a jackrabbit barely escaping a cougar. Sheer terror floods and energises any prey animal when danger comes this close. But they do not seem to be traumatised. Safe in their burrow, they will shake, twitch and vibrate, often for several minutes, as they discharge the adrenaline created. And then, they move on.

But in our present culture, we humans are so trained to repress our Wild Creature responses that most of us have accumulated lots of 'unfinished business'; emotions and hurts that stay in our system, unexpressed. This means that when we encounter similar situations again, the well-known phenomena of 'triggering' can happen. This isn't something to avoid or be annoyed about. It's an invitation to explore – when you have the time – and complete what is needing to be completed. (We'll explore how to do this in Chapter 9.)

Our Wild Creature can seem overreactive, and it may be that you have to soothe it. For example, you may be frightened by turbulence on an airline flight, which certainly *feels* dangerous. So you need to reassure yourself with the statistics on airline safety (left brain can sometimes use logic to soothe right brain). Or we can use animal friendly methods – we use slow breathing to calm down, or comfort ourselves with a hot chocolate or a warm bath. One trick to let go of a panic attack is to tighten up the big muscles of your arms and legs, and hold them for ten seconds or so, several times over. (It's less noticeable if you just do one arm or leg at a time!) The large muscles then pump blood back to your core and make your body think it has outrun the lion, and it noticeably settles. (This has got me through some very hairy plane trips in remote parts of the world!)

You can soothe your Wild Creature, just as you would a pet or a small child. But you shouldn't just ignore its signals; you still need to figure out what is behind its restlessness or alarm. The secret is to dialogue with it until you get to the bottom of why it is reacting as it is. Not by rationalising (or gaslighting yourself), but really sitting with that bodily discomfort until there is a shift and you know where it comes from.

You will find yourself using Wild Creature felt sense more and more as you progress. Why is there a strange clench down low in your stomach on just one side as you drive to the airport? You slow down and pay attention to it, and bingo, a memory suddenly pops into your head – a picture of yourself packing your passport in your *check-in* luggage (true life story, don't ask). Or a new person you have met makes you feel tight in the throat (and not in a good way!). You quietly sit with that, and there it is again, just popping into your mind – the image of someone who hurt you, years ago. Is this person going to do the same? Perhaps not, but you know what to watch out for. It's worthy of going carefully.

And finally, Wild Creature Mind is not just about problems. It will lead you to good places too. When we let our Wild Creature feel and enjoy, things just go better – more fun, more laughter and delight.

Summing Up

You will now be getting the concept that you have two minds, and one of them is nonverbal and draws on complex information largely out of awareness. To begin with, its felt sense language is always 'fuzzy', and we have to dialogue with it to find what it is trying to say.

You will recognise it by its qualities – it is subtle, fresh and unique, changing every second. (If it feels the same, you are not paying enough attention.) And it has a totality about it – it sums up the 'everything' of a situation, even when something is very complex. You can ask it, 'How do I feel about *all* of this?' and it tells you straight away. It specialises in the executive summary.

Tapping into our Wild Creature doesn't mean abandoning our logical grasp of the world. We humans have things that other wild creatures do not – notably language, and abstract thought. Abstract thought is helpful in a world that changes, and wild creatures suffer when they cannot use it. Instinct can fail them, so they eat plastic or mistake city lights for the moon and become fatally lost. We humans acquired language and abstract thought as a way to help our lives, and it certainly did, but it also came at a cost.

A new skill takes practice, but not the 'furrowed brow' kind of effortful practice. This one works best if you just gently show some curiosity and playfully experiment.

At the very least, it can mean you have a whole new resource to help you get comfortable in your own skin, and with others around you. At *best*, it can help you finally know who you really are, that you finally belong in the world and are part of making the future a better place. For us and all the other wild creatures.

Felt sense is a force beyond thought which nonetheless shapes the living world. It stops the lion in its tracks and lifts the shore bird into the air. It brings the great flocks of grazing beasts on the Serengeti into migration. It draws the teenager out of their parents' house on a warm summer evening and into a larger world.

Chapter 7

Eugene Gendlin and the Bridge Between the Minds

Two men pore over a reel-to-reel tape recorder in a quiet university room. The year is 1958. One man is in his fifties, the other his thirties. The older, Carl Rogers, has an illustrious career unfolding. He will soon come to outrank Sigmund Freud in lists of the most influential therapists of history. Within a decade, there will be basically two kinds of psychotherapists – Freudians and Rogerians.

But it's his younger colleague we are interested in. Eugene Gendlin, a Jewish Austrian refugee who arrived in America in January 1939. As a PhD student in the philosophy department of the University of Chicago, he has sought out Rogers to add psychology to his palette. He must have been an impressive student because in years to come, he collaborates with Rogers and influences his work to a surprising degree.

Rogers has already turned the world of therapy on its head. He has declared war on the psychoanalysts, not by direct attack but by going against all their basic precepts. He does not believe in the authority of the analyst; he sees therapy as a *partnership of equals*. He does not see people as patients and refuses to medicalise or label their sufferings with a diagnosis or category. He rarely if ever gives advice, or even interpretation, though he does point out gently when words and action do not match. Rogers respects his patients as equals at a time when the medical profession is still parading patients in front of interns and sharing case notes like baseball cards.

Rogers listens. He has discovered something really important – that when someone comes in seeking help, they naturally tell their story and how they see the problem. The therapist attempts to check their understanding, to sum up the problem. In the first attempt, the therapist is never quite correct, so the client corrects them. Gradually, the client and therapist arrive at a shared narrative rather than some interpretation imposed by the therapist to fit their pet theories. Importantly, the story becomes clearer in the client's mind. They may never have laid it out before another human being in quite this way, and already they are feeling more objective and empowered. Surprise, surprise (as my old dad used to say), when treated with respect, genuine interest and accurate empathy (not gooey, fake sympathy), the client starts to feel able to take on their life with new strength. Or new softness, if that was what was missing.

In the buttoned-up world of the 1950s – with its repression of emotions and of even standard sexuality let alone diverse forms, its judgemental, sexist, racist norms – this was wild stuff. Most clients had never experienced such acceptance and space to be their true selves.

Perhaps most outrageously for the psychoanalysts, Rogers does not see counselling as the preserve of professionals. Out of his work will arise all the things we take for granted today – volunteer telephone hotlines, shopfront counselling centres, school counsellors, ministers trained in pastoral care. Anyone who cares for others can, when needed, take a counselling role, and gain the same skills – or better – than the men with couches and notebooks.

While this humanistic psychology revolution is impressive, not everyone responds to counselling. The failures and the successes are about fifty-fifty, worryingly close to random. And so Rogers, Gendlin and their team listen to recordings, clipboards in hand, and read hundreds of transcripts to find out what makes the difference.

And they find it.

In short, Gendlin and Rogers discover that there are two distinct kinds of people who come for therapy. One kind has an absolute commitment to their side of the story. They tell a tale of misfortune or persecution then fold their arms and say, 'See?' In a sense, they aren't looking for change, but for vindication. (I am being a little unkind here, but on the best interpretation, they are not able to see any other way of looking at their problems.) Their hearts are not open to change, and so they rarely do. Today, we would add that this is very much affected by the qualities of the therapist, since we are really talking about trust. Hearts open when they feel other hearts caring, and that is not something that can be taught in a lecture room.

With the clients who benefit and recover, what is striking is how similar it is in every case. Some way into the first session, the therapist asks a question that is a little more probing, and the client pauses and stops talking. They seem to go inside themselves, and search. After a moment or two, they say that they don't exactly know, but, 'It's something like this . . . No, that isn't quite it, it's more this . . .' In short, these clients grope about for a new understanding, one which does not come from thinking, but from 'sensing'. In other words, as you are bound to be observing, they consult their Wild Creature Mind.

Gendlin describes this moment as 'the fuzzy edge'. That before any change can come, there has to be:

1. A searching inside.
2. A sense of something undefined but definitely 'there' – a *physical sense* of the presence of some new answer.
3. Searching for the right word or 'handle' to capture the quality of the felt sense. Usually, it takes several tries, as the two hemispheres of the brain work to understand each other.
4. Finally, the client hits upon a word or phrase that fits. And when that is hit on, the body itself seems to say, 'Yes.' And there is a shift.
5. With the two hemispheres now in open and conscious communication, there is both a new insight or aware-ness about the problem, and a confirming solidness, settling or softening in the felt sense as a solution has started to emerge. To paraphrase the shampoo ad, it might not happen straight away, but it's begun.

As Gendlin always emphasised, this is simply a natural process of the human mind. It is how we are meant to work. It's restoring full functioning, even if only momentarily. Gendlin and Rogers did not invent this; they discovered its existence. Any human being can do it.

Rogers will move on from this, but Gendlin is hooked. He is a philosopher and he knows that the mind is a thing in motion. It is built to go forwards, and never stops growing and 'improving'. We just have to give it our attention and it will lead us somewhere new. *It has the answers*. One part of us knows what the other part is so desperate to find out. We just have to get those parts talking.

Gendlin will develop this idea into a whole field of therapy called 'focusing', though I always found that an unsatisfactory name for something so potent. He and his partner, Mary Hendricks Gendlin, will carry it through into use in science, noting that all researchers, whether in engineering, genetics, medicine or whatever, have a 'sense' of an answer just out of reach, of something that exists but is still needing to be found. That if they learn to 'think at the edge', they can turbocharge their thinking by using their right brain's grasp of the nonlinear totality, which a logical mind could only follow like a skier behind a speedboat.

How Does it Work?

'But wait,' you will be saying, 'how does the focusing actually work? How does it help us to "find the words" that fit the sensation?' Sensations in our body are not a frozen thing, like a dislocated shoulder. They are a stirring of some kind of message our right hemisphere is wanting us to hear, a journey it wants to take us on. When we search for language (left brain) to describe felt sense (right brain), it sparks something between the two sides. Something starts to change in both, at the same time; thinking and felt sense release something in each other.

In striving to find the words to describe the felt sense, we activate both our left and right hemispheres at the same time. We create a 'relationship' between them of curious openness, and so the Wild Creature part of us becomes more expansive. I can't explain it more than that, except to say, you can feel it when you do it, and it's a rather surprising, even exhilarating thing. Gendlin always talks about how 'intricate', 'fresh' and 'specific' these signals in our body really are. These signals are very different to the blunt instruments of emotion, they are like delicate writings on our consciousness, hinting at what we need to do and where we need to go next. Reading novels, movies, poetry, music, art, travel, dance, or just going for a walk on the beach are other ways that we get our Wild Creature to talk to us. We do these things for *what they stir in us.*

In my book *Fully Human*, I told a personal story of this sudden linkage between left-brain understanding, and what our Wild Creature Mind is trying to tell us. In our early thirties, Shaaron and I suffered a miscarriage, and I fell into a deep depression which I couldn't find a way out of.

To my astonishment, after several months of this getting steadily worse, I one day sat with my guitar and began to play randomly. Then, suddenly a song came into my head and as I remembered the words I began weeping. The song was 'Ruby Tuesday', about a girl who went away, and with my tears came a sudden flash of insight – the realisation that on some unconscious level, I had hoped for this baby to have been a *daughter*. Once the two sides of my brain were swapping this information, I could both feel what I needed to, and know the reason why. And it was music that made the connection. Music exists because it evokes feeling, and helps us to be alive to our own insides. We are amazingly made, and the more we understand this, the less we have to suffer needlessly. There is enough real suffering in life, without adding to it by having a frozen heart. Suffering, if we can stay open to it, joins us to life, and there is a clear free place beyond it.

An Idea Whose Time Has Come

Focusing therapists today are a worldwide network, a rather amazing bunch. They have that European commitment to intellectual rigour combined with the deep roots in philosophy bequeathed by Gendlin. But they are also very grounded, and so present in their bodies that they seem to radiate aliveness.

The ideas of focusing are also to be found in many other modalities – I learned them without knowing their name when I trained as a Gestalt therapist in the 1980s. They underpin Somatic Experiencing, the current promising approach to trauma therapy, which we will visit in Chapter 12. They are a key component of Internal Family Systems therapy, which is now very popular among therapists in Australia. Gendlin taught that you can improve any counselling or therapy method – even the more wooden ones like CBT – simply by asking at key times whether the person can 'feel inside themselves and describe what is going on'. And, by doing so, they can go beyond thought, below mere emotions and directly experience the growing edge of their own process, where change takes place. Thoughts in our left hemisphere come and go; they have all the durability of a New Year's resolution. But when something anchored by the deep structure of the right hemisphere shifts, and is felt in the body, your life has changed.

Building bridges to our Wild Creature Mind, by checking in with it routinely and carefully as often as we can, rewires our brain. It is direct neurosurgery without the need for a scalpel, getting right to where the answers lie. It makes other therapies look rather lame.

Gendlin discovered 'felt sense'. He wasn't too concerned about how it worked. That would come only after he died, with the work of Iain McGilchrist and the neuroscientists, who would prove him to have been right. He provided the flesh, and McGilchrist the bones. We owe a great debt to them both.

THE RIGHT HEMISPHERE HAS ITS OWN MAP OF THE BODY

Something we didn't mention until now – the right hemisphere actually has an inbuilt three-dimensional representation of the whole body. (It's in the somato-sensory cortex, and the motor cortex, to be technical.) It represents our whole body, especially its sensory aspects. There is still some uncertainty about whether Gendlin's felt sense actually occurs down in our torso (where we feel it to be), or in the brain's representation of our torso, since there is really no way we can differen-tiate this subjectively. But it is likely to be a combination of both. This is why when we check in with our felt sense, and welcome it, muscles twitch or relax, our stomach often gurgles, or we burp or have a mighty yawn, or indigestion or heart tension go away. And why trembling or shuddering can bring mental resolution and even new thoughts. We think with our muscles too.

IT HELPS TO HAVE HELP

Gendlin was strongly of the view that doing focusing on your own is often a bit of a struggle, especially if the issues have some pain or complexity behind them. Having a focusing partner has become a practice for many people – both therapists for their own maintenance, and lots of other people who have found the method so transformative that they want to build it into their lives. The International Focusing Institute offers basic training courses for this, and help with partnering with another person (often on the other side of the world). This can become a long-term partnership – in fact, most do.

They do this as a natural form of maintenance and growth, and find it a fantastic way of staying clear and free. Each person takes a turn – half an hour – to go inside themself and track down issues and concerns, while the other acts as a respondent. Then you reverse roles and do the same for them. It's a brilliant help in living your life, costs nothing and is very egalitarian. You might want to look on the focusing.org website, there is also a vast amount of helpful material freely available there.

The reason a person helping you matters is because it is easier to dive into your own right hemisphere–body experience if someone else takes over for your left hemisphere. The role of a focusing partner (or therapist) is to entirely desist from any direction/interpretation, and simply echo back to you the progress you are making. So that when one reports, 'There is a kind of tightness in my throat', they will probably just repeat, 'A tightness in your throat.' This would be annoying in a lunchroom conversation, but when you are journeying into your inner world, it is exactly what you need; it holds you to the awareness and so you move to the next step. You report on an uncomfortable feeling in your throat as you talk about your fear of public speaking.

'Choking, it's kind of choking me.'

Your partner echoes, 'Kind of choking you.'

And you suddenly get a deeper sense of what your Wild Creature is doing. 'It wants to keep me from speaking.' And then, 'It wants to save me from getting into trouble' and suddenly one is face-to-face with Wild Creature protectiveness, and you can negotiate with it and find a way to make that wedding speech after all! (That's half an hour squashed into six lines, but you get the idea.)

When you are helping a child, a friend or a therapy client in this way, you do very little, but it's absolutely the best help you can give.

How to Know Your Boundaries – and Guard Them

One of the easiest and most important uses of Wild Creature awareness is in setting boundaries. Knowing where our boundaries are (what to say yes to and what to say no to) is a huge problem for at least one in three people. It is vital for protecting our mental health, wellbeing, safety and self-respect. Boundaries save us from overcommitment, over entanglement and all the other 'overs' that can steal our freedom and joy.

Many people think that their tendency to be a pushover is some kind of character weakness, but it's really just a simple thing of knowing how to listen to your insides! Your thinking mind may be wavering and in doubt, but boundaries are not a matter of just thinking. They are something you just know in the domain of your Wild Creature Mind. (Wild animals never doubt their boundaries.) Through your Wild Creature Mind's super sensing of subtle cues ('That person feels creepy', 'This request is manipulative', 'This person is just asking too much') and its high-speed deep access to your lifetime of memories, it has already decided. You just have to hear its voice.

People who are good at setting boundaries are not 'stronger' than you; they just do two simple things that you can do too.

If someone asks them to do something, they first allow themselves a strategic pause, so as to consider their answer. It might be just a few seconds, or it might be, 'Let me get back to you when I have had a think/checked my diary/ sorted a few things out.'

Secondly, in that strategic pause, they access Wild Creature signals in their body, to know what they really want. If you are out of practice at knowing your own wishes, it may be faint at first. On page 271, we have a whole six exercises to help you acquire this skill. Of course, sometimes those signals will be flashing amber lights, like an 80s disco! You know what you want, and you have the claws ready to guard it.

With Wild Creature help, the mildest and gentlest of us can be fierce. Here is a story to prove it.

GET READY TO BE OUTRAGED, AND INSPIRED . . .
Mary Hendricks Gendlin, wife of Eugene Gendlin, told this story at a World Focusing Conference, Berlin, 2003. At 1:23 on a Saturday afternoon a perfect baby girl was born to her parents after a short, uncomplicated labour. She was

born in a birthing room at a modern suburban hospital in mid-America. Her mother and she, being free of drugs, took a long deep look at each other, bonding for life.

The father rushed back to work to conclude a large presentation. The pediatrician the family had selected was not on-call. His partner filled in. The mother was told by a nurse, 'The baby is a bit jaundiced. The doctor wants you to stay overnight in the hospital so we can keep an eye on her.' Upstairs on the ward, a few hours later, a technician came into the room and took several vials of blood from the baby's heel. The baby cried out each time.

A few hours later, another technician appeared, needle and vial in hand.

Mother: 'What are you doing?'

Technician: 'We need to take blood for some tests.'

Mother: 'Wait a minute. Stop. You just took her blood. What is this test for?'

Technician: 'To check on the jaundice.'

Mother: 'Wait. I need to think about this. (She is quiet for a minute.) If the results of this test are positive, then what follows from that?'

Technician: 'Then we wait twelve hours and repeat the test.'

Mother: 'Humm. (Quiet again.) So why do we need to do the test now, if the only result is that you wait twelve hours and repeat it?'

Technician: 'To keep track of what is going on.'

Mother: 'We will wait twelve hours and then I will consider whether to do the test then.'

Technician: 'But the doctor ordered it now.'

Mother: 'I'm sorry, you do not have my permission to do any more tests on my baby.'

An uproar ensued. The mother, quite tired from having just given birth and trying to learn how to breast-feed her baby, was visited by a stream of technicians, floor nurses and others. Most said, 'You should do what the doctor orders!' A few said, 'Good for you. You do what seems right to you.'

At about 9 pm, the pediatrician called the mother in her room.

Doctor: 'If you don't have the tests I ordered, then I cannot be responsible for your baby.'

Mother: 'I agree. You are no longer responsible for her. I no longer wish to work with you.'

The mother called another pediatrician, who came early the next morning, examined the baby and said, 'She is fine. You can go home.'

As the family prepared to leave, one of the nurses said, 'Dr _____ is doing research on jaundice in babies. He does blood tests on all the babies, for his research.'

Everything pivoted on those two moments where Mary gave herself permission to go inside herself and see what felt right. What Wild Creature was telling her. She was vulnerable, exhausted, and being bullied.

When we become a parent, a part of us comes alive which would kill with our bare hands, if that is what it took to protect our child. You just have to go look for it. It will be there.

Summing Up

We now have the whole picture in place. McGilchrist and the several thousand brain studies he draws on make clear the existence of our Wild Creature Mind, centred in one half of our brain, and interwoven through our body. Literally 'every fibre of our being'! But McGilchrist gives little indication of how we are to talk to it.

A sweet, avuncular philosopher with twinkling eyes, Gendlin provides the method, and two worlds collide. The practitioners of focusing evolved a way of listening to the body, which is intricate, elegant and powerful. In the fuzzy edge between the minds, dialogue is possible; and going inside ourselves can tell us what we need to know. The Wild Creature is suddenly right there alongside us, bursting with life.

And off we go.

Chapter 8

How Your Wild Creature Heals You

When we last saw him, James had used his newly learned skill for the first time, to settle his anxiety and get some much-needed sleep. But that is only the very edge of what he needs. For James (and probably for you, dear reader, and for almost everyone reading this), there is a great deal that has gone before that needs to be untangled. Care and attention will be needed to find out what is really devastating his mental health and bring it into the sunlight, where it can heal.

James is incredibly lucky in his choice of therapist, as we will soon see. But first, let us get a grounded understanding of what is going on inside anyone who suffers from post-traumatic injury.

The understanding is finally out in our culture: that we can carry unfinished and quite severe emotional after-effects of bad things we've been through. We even have a slightly playful word for it – 'baggage'. But though we joke about it, the fact is that the sheer weight of baggage so many people are carrying is messing with our world. Trauma not addressed tends to compound and be inflicted down the generations. If you have ever asked yourself why it is that our world is such a nightmare of violence, war and self-destructive impulses, large and small, this probably the reason. The history of the modern world is defined by intergenerational trauma. Or more accurately, *unresolved* trauma.

But why does our mind do this to us in the first place? The answer is all about how our two minds were designed to work, and how we have let that amazing biological system fall into disuse.

Here's a simple example.

A little toddler crushes their finger in a closing door. They scream and cry, and their mother comforts them, cuddling them, making soothing noises. 'Ooh that hurt, that was a big shock! I'm here, it's alright.' The child cries, then quietens, then cries a bit more, gradually calming. Even so, hours later, they tell their grandma all about it, and their big brother when he gets back from school. Only then is the child finally settled.

Their right hemisphere is letting go of the physical pain. Wild Creature Mind knows that making a lot of noise somehow reduces the physical pain. (As adults we might instead choose to let go a string of profanities!) The yelling or crying lets the adrenaline run its course, but their animal mind also stores 'Doors can hurt you!' with a big red flag in its memory banks. And finally, well, that was the worst pain I ever felt, but I got through it. How interesting!

At the same time, their left hemisphere is making sense of it in words. 'This is a thing that can happen, but the door doesn't chase you, you just have to keep your fingers clear!' Both hemispheres combine to get this child back in balance.

What if its more severe? A twelve-year-old learns on returning from the holidays that one of their schoolfriends has died in an accident. They spend the day in stunned silence, but when their dad picks them up after school, they burst into tears.

On and off they cry many times in the next few days. It is the first experience in their life of a real person dying. Part of them can't believe it. The memorial service helps, a little, to be in 'shared upset' with others, and to value that friend's life and memory. But it takes many weeks, being quiet and reflective, noticing their tendency to 'fly off the handle' as bits of the shock filter though. Almost every emotion is involved. The young person makes room for new sensations in their body, and the body does its work of repair. Anyone who has experienced profound grief is shocked at how very physical it is, how much it just *hurts*. Wild Creature Mind and left hemisphere pass the reality of death and loss to-and-fro, edging towards healing. Gradually the young person emerges, enlarged and more appreciative of friends and family, and being alive in the world, from this first real encounter with death.

Having hard things happen needn't harm us, in fact humans were designed for trauma, in the sense that pre-historic life was always fraught. And we evolved, like all animals, ways to use both hemispheres to process it. Crying, shaking, wailing, raging, talking.

But what if this wasn't allowed? Imagine if you hit your hand with a hammer, but were not allowed to yell or swear? If your sister or brother died, and nobody was allowed to ever mention them again. (I have had patients where this did happen.) No grief, no funeral, no remembrance. So no place for your right hemisphere's bodily healing processes to take place. You would be like a walking time bomb of unexpressed, uncomprehending derangement. Your two hemispheres would not be on speaking terms, lest they unleash the pain you've been forbidden to show. In a sense, this is what happened in our history. Westerners conquered the natural world and we silenced our own wildness. It was a terrible act of self-mutilation. Iain McGilchrist's message, and mine too, is that we can get this back. And it isn't even really that hard.

So let's pick up James's story. James got a good night's sleep after tuning into his body sensations and accepting them, delineating them and letting the two sides of his brain communicate just for a moment or two. But that, of course, was only a short-term fix. The next day, he is still unsettled and anxious, as he has in fact been for many months. Policemen, soldiers, emergency workers and health workers of every kind are exposed to strong emotions so often in their jobs that their Wild Creature is hammered and has a lot of catching up to do. It has a lot to say.

A Turning Point

James has his next appointment with his counsellor several days later. Ange is a woman in her late fifties, tall, with a thoughtful, expressive face. James has observed that she favours unfussy comfortable clothing, her face is tanned and she seems at ease in her body. There is both an informality yet a laser-like focus in her manner. In short, he likes her and has come to trust her after initial misgivings about the whole idea.

As soon as they have settled into their chairs, he tells her that the method she taught him was helpful in getting to sleep. She smiles, and says, 'Well done. You are a fast learner.'

He smiles.

Then she asks, 'So how are you now?'

'Well . . . still the same, to be honest. Edgy. My wife says I am "spaced out" at home, mentally hardly there. I don't talk much.'

'Sure. So we've got work to do!' She settles lower in her seat and meets his gaze, taking him in. Her expression is kind, but full of intent. 'So, get in touch with your body, settle into being here in this room, and feel your weight in the chair . . .'

She pauses, waiting for him to start getting aware, drop down from the social performing effort we all make when with another person, and tune into ourselves. After a few seconds, she asks, 'What do you notice in your body?' She gestures with her hand down her own midline as she speaks.

He hesitates a second and then tells her, 'I'm tight around my heart.'

'Okay. Just notice that, what it's doing, what the quality of it is.' A pause. 'What else do you notice?'

'I'm quite hot, up around my chest. My heart is racing a bit.'

'That's great. Just let that be there. Make it welcome.'

James struggles for a second or two with this idea of welcome. He doesn't *like* having body symptoms which, if he was to characterise them at all, would be failings, weaknesses, like something going wrong. For a moment, he is a bit shocked at how cross he is with himself and has a second go at welcoming this bundle of symptoms, at least open to the possibility that it has something to offer him.

Ange has told him a little about the neuroscience in his early sessions, that we have parts of our mind trying to get our attention, and that body sensations are how our right brain tries to help us. He trusts science – he's a paramedic after all – and he is motivated to learn, especially if it can prevent him from disintegration, from losing a career he started out really loving.

He softens in both his attitude and his actual musculature around his heart and chest, and Ange, who has crouched forwards and is watching intently, makes an affirming sound beloved of counsellors.

'Mmmhhmm. You're doing great.'

Part of him is impressed that she can see his inner processes through close observation.

'What is happening now?' she asks.

He is suddenly aware of a movement upwards from his chest, which has softened a little, to his throat, as if a murky sphere of something intangible is rising inside him.

'My throat feels strange, like a big lump.'

He is uncomfortable, a bit rattled, while at the same time rather captivated that just talking in a quiet room is having so much effect.

'What are you noticing now?' she asks again.

Ange has moved slightly forwards. Her chair has wheels and, while not crowding him, she finds just the right distance so he feels she is intently with him. There is a protective quality to her whole demeanour, like a mother to a small child, but not patronising; watchful, waiting.

'My throat,' he says. His voice catches as he says it. 'It's really tight.'

Ange breathes in and out herself, taking her time. 'As you are breathing in and out, on the out breath, start to just make a bit of a sound, like an "Aahhh". Whatever sound seems to come . . .'

He tentatively does so. 'Aahhh.' It's caught, gravelly, strangled-sounding.

'Soften your throat; let the sound come out more strongly.'

'Aahhh . . .'

And with that, James feels a rush of tears. Inside, on some level, he consents, allowing them to come. He knows that he could choke the tears back, but that is no longer what he wants to do. In seconds, great heaving sobs are coming from deep down in his belly and out of his throat and eyes. Half of him is dismayed, embarrassed; the other half knows this is a breakthrough.

Curved forwards so his head is bent over his knees, he sobs. Ange wheels closer to him in her chair, not touching him, just present, making affirming sounds. Then he feels her hand gently on his foot, on his shoe, anchoring him. The effect is to let even more sobbing come out of his body from some deep place inside him.

When the body has 'stored' strong feelings, the natural healing process is frozen. A young widow 'carries on' for her children's sake when every part of her wants to just collapse in grief. A child sexually abused by a family member holds in the shame, disgust and sheer agony of their young body, and acts like a perfect child. We soldier on. But one day, these blocked processes of healing have to be let go if we are to ever experience wholeness or happiness. To love with an open heart or trust and feel safe.

Ange waits patiently for James to process what has just happened, the sudden release of anguish that so far has no explanation, but is clearly huge. She breathes slowly to calm herself too, and be peaceful amid such turbulence.

James's head rises a little, not yet meeting her gaze, but becoming more present in the room.

Ange's next question is phrased in a way that still directs him to his own inner process. 'What are you experiencing?'

He hesitates a second, but the answer is already there in his left hemisphere. 'Karina.'

Ange simply says, 'Yes?'

'She was a little girl. A patient.'

This is not easy for James. These are thoughts and facts that he has not spoken of ever to anyone. There is a pain in his face, and he seems on the brink of weeping again.

Ange keeps him on the thread of thought, firmly in his logical side now.

'What happened, James?'

Her voice is soft, registering that this is huge, that he has her full attention.

In the half hour that follows, James tells Ange that Karina was a four-year-old girl hit by a car going too fast in a bus zone outside her preschool. Excited and distracted, emerging from behind a stationary bus, she had seen her mum across the road and – well, we don't need to go there. James and his co-driver's ambulance had been there in eleven minutes. The child was still conscious, but her injuries grave. He remembers saying to the child and to her mum, 'You are going to be okay, we will take care of you,' driving with sirens at full speed and then his partner hefting himself forwards into the cab, giving him a look. *Too late.*

When this harrowing story is over, both James and his counsellor are silent.

'What is coming into your mind now, James?' Ange has to make herself keep breathing, noticing she had barely done so for several minutes.

'I told her we would take care of her.'

'And what do you think as you think about that?'

'That there wasn't anything we could have done. *She was never going to make it.*'

Ange takes a stab. It isn't a therapist's job to be right, but to be willing to have a go. 'You feel badly about what you said?'

'Yes. No. You just say things, there isn't time to think.'

'It seems a good thing to say, to reassure a little child?'

'I guess. I just . . . her injuries, her mum . . . seeing it all happen. It was terrible.'

'Yes. And it needed someone to show up in the ambulance and do their best.'

'Yeah. We got her morphine, we worked to stop the bleeding. We were fast.'

There is a silence, ten, fifteen seconds, then Ange speaks. 'And sometimes, it's just too late.'

'Yes.'

A week later, on a sunny cold morning, James and Ange meet at the cemetery where Karina is buried. Ange greets James and tells him she will wait at a distance. She perches on a convenient grave, matter-of-fact, but with sadness on her face.

James has flowers. He walks the fifty metres to Karina's small gravestone.

He is there for a time, crouched down. Then he actually sits on the ground and begins to say something. Tears stream down his face as he tells Karina that he is sorry he could not save her. He asks her forgiveness, knowing this isn't in any way logical, but that it feels right. Something in him needs to do it.

His face, when he comes back to Ange, has regained its colour. He moves with a softness and care, glancing about at the trees and a flurry of birds going by. Ange does something she has never done with him before – she extends an arm and he folds into a warm long hug.

They exchange a few sentences. Both smile slightly, breathing full, deep breaths. They get into their separate cars and Ange drives slowly off. James sits for a time, and then is ready to take himself home.

Summing Up

Trauma has always been part of human life. And so we evolved methods to process it, to heal and move on. It needn't be a life sentence. A natural process has been interrupted, and that process can be restarted. The acute symptoms we sometimes feel – like out of control anxiety, intrusive thoughts, explosive feelings – are not malfunctions in our body or brain. They are our Wild Creature Mind trying to get us well again. If we are given ordinary human support, with care and attention to where our body is guiding us, then we can find answers and bring resolution.

Our present self is an expression of what has gone wrong, as well as right, in our lives and both are equally what make us beautiful and worthwhile. When we have both halves of our mind working together, they move quickly and elegantly towards resolution, as they have done in animals for millions of years. So we can get on with being alive. We are amazing because of, not in spite of, all we have learned and come through. We are better for it. Better able to care and to love.

NOT A PROBLEM – BUT A JOURNEY

There is something which those who have never experienced good therapy might find surprising – it's the sense of relief and support which settles on your whole life, knowing there is someone you can tell anything to, who won't give up on you and is on your side. (Even though they may also kick your backside when you deserve it.)

In other words, when a person is 'in counselling', if the bond and trust are good, then that presence extends beyond the therapy room. The patient feels accompanied, in a good way, as they now go about their life. There are two specific changes which counselling triggers. The first is the sense that they are *not alone*; that everything unfolding can be discussed, figured out and the burden can be shared. For a person who has always felt they are struggling alone, often for as long as they can remember, this is an immense change.

The second change, closely tied to the first, is that they are defining their time now as *a healing journey*. A story is unfolding which is towards life being better, perhaps even transformed. What might have felt like setbacks are more clearly reframeable as new layers lifting off, as grist for the mill, and a neurological process has been triggered towards better integration of all their disparate, traumatised or warring parts. The ethos of therapy is clear – *a person heals themself*, just as they do with a physical disease, but the presence of a safeguarding guide alongside them means there need be fewer reversals and no harm. When they feel stuck, they can get unstuck. And the messages of the body are always the key. What another caring human being can provide is the sense of safety to go into places that were not safe before.

So for you, dear reader, do take on board that this is not just a self-help book, because how humans really grow is 'each-other-help'. Helping each other is the core fact of being human. On our own, we can only go so far.

EXERCISES: FIRST AID

Sometimes your left brain is just in such a spin, and you haven't got quite the presence of mind to do the proper 'There is something in me' process. It is possible to downregulate your system with one of these gentle interventions to get on a calmer footing short term . . .

1. Humming: Take a breath in, and then on the out breath do a long even hum, the same note, for as long as your breath will go. Repeat a few times, if needed. Peter Levine uses a 'vooo' sound but that just makes me laugh. Which is okay too! Some people have a small tremor in their body at the end of the hum, which is their body letting go, so it's a good sign.

2. Square breathing: This just means you breath in, hold, breath out, hold, for approximately the same amount of time. I find that the out breaths get longer, and that seems to help.

3. If you are somewhere still – in bed or seated somewhere private – tense up your arms and legs as tightly as you can and hold for as long as is comfortable and then release. Pay attention to the sensations that come when you release, and let them spread into the rest of you.

But always, when you can, use 'There is something in me'. Even if you haven't got time for dialogue, your Wild Creature responds positively to being noticed.

Chapter 9

The Shift

Sometimes in life, we have breakthroughs.

I am sure you have experienced this. You've been going along in a rut, feeling increasingly unhappy with something, or even with *everything* in your life. And then, one day a light goes on, you see with new clarity, and you just *change*. It can be a small thing or it can be huge. I was once walking in another city and a woman in her sixties walked over to me with a warm smile. 'It's Steve isn't it? I was on one of your courses in the 1980s. After that weekend, I realised my marriage was crushing me, and I left. And my job was terrible, so I changed careers. And finally, I saw that I had a bad relationship with alcohol, so I got help for that. So, thank you!' And she touched my arm gently, beamed a smile with lighthouse-intensity and was on her way.

My social cogs always turn slowly, especially when taken by surprise. But standing there watching her go I did have a big smile. And I did remember her, I could picture where she sat in the room in that Adult Education course. She had barely spoken a word the whole weekend!

It is the nature of the mind to stabilise, find a pattern and keep it. When we change, we tend to do it all at once, neural dominoes just start to fall. So any personal breakthrough is exhilarating to witness or to experience. Think of your favourite movie, and these will always be the climactic and best bits – often right at the end. (*The Bodyguard* has a cracker of a finish. And there is an episode of *The West Wing*, the one where they play 'Brothers in Arms'. Showing my vintage here!)

Once, long ago, I wrote a book called *Manhood: An action plan for changing men's lives*. Sick of those unhelpful articles about the masculinity crisis, I went for solutions, and there were plenty. One was Robert Bly's message that we'd all survived a massive father wound, which ran like the Grand Canyon through the 20th century via endless wars and mass industrialisation. The emotional or often actual disappearance of men from children's lives had crippled us all, but especially boys. Then there was the enslavement of the average man, giving his life to a corporation in exchange for the love of a woman and the privilege of having a home and family.

When I spoke about the father wound in my live shows, men would weep openly, it was so personal and intense. In the years following *Manhood*'s publication, thousands of men took the path of reconciliation with old or dying dads. And an uncounted number of readers – men (and some women too) – took the job provocation, and walked away from faceless jobs to do what they really wanted. From these personal breakthroughs, kids and partners benefitted from having a father who was not a gutted shell of himself. Warmer, more open-hearted men emerged and a new kind of masculinity began to gain momentum.

The Inside and the Outside Meet

The message here is that, in a lifetime focused on creating change, *I have never changed anyone.* I have only triggered something people knew, deep inside, and they were then able to act on it.

Breakthroughs are the core purpose of therapy, too. We work to help our clients find the breakthrough understanding that makes everything change. A suicidal person commits to staying alive. Violent men (or women) realise what they are doing and get help to stop. Greedy rich people become philanthropists and change thousands of lives. Bitter people decide not to be.

So the question is: since we all need these breakthrough moments in order to grow, how can we bring them about? How can we stop going in circles?

Change Comes from Inside

Big changes rarely come from being directed by someone else. The biggest myth about therapy – fostered on both sides of the room – is that after hearing your problem, this 'qualified expert' will provide an amazing insight which you yourself have not known because you are dull and thick. The therapist has a 'magic bullet' and they shoot you with it!

Now, just occasionally, this can be true. Sometimes we can really be blind to ourselves. Sometimes a person is just such an ass that it shows in five minutes, and a brave therapist can tactfully tell them, 'No wonder you can't keep a partner. You are rude and selfish! But I'm sure you don't mean to be. Would you like some help with that?'

But this is rare. What actually creates the best change is a therapist – or anyone, really – who brings us into *connection with ourselves*. They connect our left hemisphere with our right.

Wild Creature Mind drives change, because it has already solved the problem, and is building up like a tectonic fault inside us, just waiting to release. There is a secret we have been keeping on ourselves, and there are bodily warning signs that can provide a pathway to opening things up. It is nearly always in plain sight – a chronically tight shoulder, a fluttering stomach, or a strong impulse to run from the room, even when we know the therapist is safe and caring. These signals are a pathway into your right hemisphere's reactions and reasons. You simply follow the steps in the focusing process of locating, describing, and staying with the changing sensations. Done with care, and with help if needed, this begins a quiet avalanche of new insights. And a release of long-held emotions. In the literature of focusing therapists, this moment is known as The Shift.

There is Always a Reason

When we first met him in Chapter 5, neither James nor his therapist knew what lay behind his anxiety and distress. For a paramedic in mid-career, there could be many traumatic incidents. Or the explanation might be that he had simply burnt out and he and his family need him to be in a less intense occupation. Or it could be the opposite – that he sees so many problems with the ambulance service that rather than quitting, he wants to seek promotion and work to improve it. Or it could be something very specific – such as a colleague who drives dangerously and who he suspects of having an alcohol problem.

Or it could be something not at all work-related; that he needs to tell his wife of a mistake he made early in their relationship, and to ask for her forgiveness.

The point is that nobody, not even James himself, knew which it was. *But his Wild Creature did*. Because its job is to order and prioritise and manage complicated things. Even if everything else on our list was contributing, his silent right hemisphere knew which one needed to be tackled first. Because the right hemisphere always works at your edge, on what comes next. What is just brimming up in *this* moment, with *this* therapist, in *this* room.

For James, as we learned, it was none of the above. It was a specific remorse/grief reaction to the death of a child with whom he had formed an intense connection for just a few tragic minutes. His bodily sensations and the support of his therapist led him to suddenly just *know*. And from that, to know what he needed to do.

A friend of mine spent three hospitalisations in a specialist unit for PTSD, and almost a decade of anguish and fear for his wife and children. The resolution point for him was when he carried out a ritual of apology for the deaths of two colleagues; deaths which he could have done nothing to prevent. The sense of guilt he felt made no sense to anyone aware of the facts, but somewhere in him, he had shouldered the blame, and needed to set it down. He is travelling really well now. But Wild Creature methods could have saved him years of searching to find exactly what was the burden he carried. You have to know what has harmed you, before you can set it down.

These methods can be momentous, but they can work for small and everyday situations too. You can use them many times a day. If you listen to your body while envisaging any dilemma or situation, new insights will pop into your head. Better perspectives or completely new solutions can arise. Nearly always when we get stuck with a decision, even as small as whether to go to the shops, our left brain sees it as an either-or, a binary situation. Your right brain casts a wider net, finds an interesting third way. It can help you feel your way through decision making. ('Why don't I want to go to the shops – what is the feeling?'

'Why do I want to go? How does that feel in my body?'
'Perhaps I am just tired or need to eat something snackish,
and then see what I feel like afterwards?') Using your body
is a way out of cognitive log jams of every kind. So, main
message: Wild Creature can handle the biggest things in
your life. And the smallest!

The Complete Process

We've been describing the process of The Shift in the
examples, but to help you get the whole picture, here is
the sequence in its complete form.

1. Get present and as grounded as you can be. Breathe
   and look around you. In Ann Weiser Cornell's words,
   'clear a space'. Or as my old mum used to say, 'Settle
   yourself down.'
2. Now, either think of the problem you are concerned
   about, or just notice that you are already in a state of
   unease, and *that* is the problem. Just notice the body
   reaction that is there when you think of that.
3. Say to yourself, inside or out loud, 'There is something
   in me . . .' and as you do that, pay attention to where
   in your body this sensation or felt sense actually lives.
   It will be vague and ill-defined. Try to delineate it,
   specifically where it is located; left side or right, front or

back, high in your torso or low? What qualities does it have? (With children, they can often draw it, and even colour it and find this really helpful.) Don't rush this, it's the pivotal step. Mentally look down at your body and picture where this upset actually lives, where you can feel it the most.

The magic of doing this is that it automatically creates an objective observer part of you, noticing another quite turbulent part of you, which is capable of sensing your Wild Creature really alive inside you, and saying hello to it. The two sides of your brain are starting a conversation.

4. Let it know that you see it, and are wanting to hear it or understand it. Send it a feeling of welcome, like a wild creature that urgently wants to help you and tell you something. (Like Lassie or Skippy trying to give you a message!)

5. Look for a verbal 'handle' on this feeling. Try some words out to see if they fit, words which seem to describe it: 'holding on', 'tight', 'a big empty hole', 'churning', 'like a hard shield' etc. Each time you try a different word, notice if the felt sense gives you a sense of 'yes' or 'no'. Do this slowly and patiently until you get a 'yes'.

6. Stay closely aware of the felt sensation and notice how it responds. If it dissolves, that is fine. Perhaps it just needed you to notice. If it stays put, alters or moves,

just notice that. Most likely, it will grow a little more distinct.

7. Watch for some kind of shift to happen. Either in your thinking, or in how you feel. For new ideas or perspectives to emerge. Notice even the slightest things. If you space out or have a sudden digression, notice that. Where does it go? How might it be important?

In doing this process, you are making the optimal conditions so that (sorry, I can't resist this) Shift Happens. Large or small, it doesn't matter; you've unblocked the logjam. Another way to see it is carefully defusing unexploded bombs that have been in your path. It just takes that level of care and attention.

As you can tell, it's a kind of conversation. It will stumble along – you are not exactly ticking boxes – and you might move up and down the list a bit. And at different times, different parts of the process are the important bits. Be reassured that your Wild Creature isn't going away; it's been waiting a long time. It's not possible to get this wrong, and you can come back to it. But soon it will bear both specific fruit as well as a growing sense of being more integrated. Your two minds will start to get along.

Here It is Again, More Simply Put . . .

1. Get as present and grounded as you can be. Breathe and look around you. Mentally 'clear a space'.

2. Now, think of the problem you are concerned about. Just notice the body reaction that is there when you think of that.

3. Say to yourself, inside or out loud, 'There is something in me . . .' and as you do that, notice more specifically where in your body this felt sense actually lives.

4. Send it a feeling of welcome, and gratitude for it wanting to help you. (Like Lassie or Skippy trying to give you a message!)

5. Try some words to describe it. It is always vague at first. Each time you try a new word, notice if the felt sense gives you a sense of 'yes' or 'no'.

6. Notice how it responds. It might dissolve. If it stays put, alters or moves, just notice that. Find new words to describe its new shape or quality.

7. Watch for some kind of shift to happen. Either in your thinking, or in how you feel. For new ideas or perspectives to emerge. The intensity might go away, meaning you have integrated its message. Or it might become more present, but in a peaceful and resolute way. You know something new about how you want to go ahead from here.

If it remains unsettling, turbulent or painful, you might have to restart the process. And of course you may need a listening friend or a therapist to help if it is just too huge. But every little step you take in befriending your Wild Creature feelings will take you forwards. It is never wasted.

Needing Help

You can find The Shift by yourself some days, but for the major roadblocks in your life, it's likely that some help will be needed. Whatever shut our Wild Creature down, at least around these big issues, was usually in our childhood, and was possibly frightening, sometimes even life-threatening. Even in warm and loving families, childhood *is* frightening sometimes. In less functional families, children often live on a knife edge. Everybody is bigger than them, and must be appeased or mollified. And sometimes – with alcohol or substance abuse for example – there are simply no rules you can rely on. We may have grown up fearing rejection by our parents or affected by their sheer ignorance, outright abusiveness or absence when we needed them the most.

So, the opposite of those nightmare conditions – someone quiet and kind, willing to sit with us patiently without judgement – makes it possible to be steady. Our Wild Creature begins to edge forwards from the dense vegetation where it's been hiding. And one day, it will step into the light.

EXERCISE: GET ALL THE ANIMALS IN THE ROOM

Ann Weiser Cornell is a warm, down-to-earth thinker and writer in the worldwide focusing community. Her online courses have been a great help to me in making Eugene Gendlin's ideas practical.

Ann believes that when we have bad experiences which are unresolved, it can split off a part of us from the whole. That part then develops a kind of life of its own, like another Wild Creature – and we can end up with a whole zoo in there. This certainly fits with the work that psychiatrist Dr George Blair–West described with his patient Jeni Haynes in her unforgettable book, *The Girl in the Green Dress*. Jeni developed over a thousand subpersonalities as a result of a nightmare childhood. Shattering our selves into subpersonalities is an extreme but life-preserving way of dealing with unbelievable trauma, especially of the long-term kind. Jeni's book is almost too horrible to read, but it is very heartening too, that some amazing people come from the worst conditions. But only if help can be brought to bear.

Multiple personality disorder is an extreme version of something that almost all of us have, in various degrees. We have different selves, it's as simple as that. Almost everyone is aware of this in themselves, but on our journey to being authentic, we might hope that one day there is just one true self, that we are made whole.

Good mental health always is about *integrating* – reaching harmony between all our parts, and one day not having separate parts. This gives us a great lead to how we can fix internal conflicts which rage in most of us, about how to feel towards those around us, how to make important choices, and so on. Wild Creature methods can be very helpful for doing this. When you are divided about what to do in any situation, try this method . . .

Whenever you are caught in a tangle, especially one that seems to persist and be intractable, it is important to separate out the subpersonalities at play.

Ann Weiser Cornell struggled with alcohol in her early years and has been brave enough to write about it. (But it could be eating, gambling or any number of behaviours that keep a person going in circles.) She noticed that she had at least three parts in her own life drama. The part that loved to drink and justified it as perfectly normal and a right to relax. A second part that hated her drinking and called her hopeless and bad. And a third part that was just so sick of this going round in circles. Untangling, which Ann now teaches as a pro-cedure, involved using Wild Creature awareness to root down inside each subpersonality and find its good and fundamental purpose. For example, the drinking side simply wanted to protect her from stress and worry, and to find a place of relief and peace. It wasn't evil or 'self-sabotaging' or any of those judgmental labels so often used. Her self-chastising side, harsh on the outside, as the 'inner critic' appears to be, was actually frightened and desperate to find safety from the chaos that drinking caused. And her frustrated part wanted the destructive cycle to end, but thought it was about willpower. Deep down, all of her parts had the same goal. But only by going deep into their sensations and bringing them into the light, could this be a felt reality. Just doing it logically is not enough.

Here is the method, for you to use in your own untangling . . .

1. Choose one point of view or side of your internal argument. Go down into your body, and find the sensations that go with that point of view. Follow the focusing sequence, trying out some words to describe the sensations, and see what comes up over a minute or so. You are looking for the fresh edge of this felt sense and what it seems to want. Remember, this is just one part of the picture, but you want to welcome it and give it some credence.

2. Now choose the other point of view and do the same thing. Don't rush it. If you have trouble staying with a felt sense, ask a friend or counsellor to help you. If there are three sides – and there usually are – don't skim over it, repeat it for the third side too.

3. Now – the interesting part. Hold in your mind the *whole experience* of having plumbed down into both

sides of this argument, what you are now feeling as a result of these last few minutes. When you reflect on 'all of that' (Gendlin's favourite phrase), what felt sense *now* comes into awareness? This will often be an entirely new sensation, the beginning of your new self, undivided and at peace. Stay with it, let it blossom. You are really getting somewhere. Yay!

In a nutshell, you resolve conflicts in yourself not by choosing one side, but by *getting inside the reasons for each* at a Wild Creature level, which is much more nuanced and profound. And then finding what new way emerges, often completely different to the choices you'd been caught up with. That beautiful expression 'the horns of a dilemma' says it all. You want to be well clear of those horns!

My clients have found this incredibly useful in dealing with those hoary conflicts that we all have of 'head versus heart'. When we frame our decisions like that, it's likely to bring us unstuck – we act 'sensibly' and walk down a path to deadness, or we act impulsively and reap the whirlwind.

But if we use our felt sense to focus down into each side – our felt sense about using our head, and our felt sense about using our heart – then we often find totally new aspects. Perhaps our head is not really our head, but our fears! Perhaps our heart is also afraid – of missing out, or being crushed by conformity. It's likely that we can steer a path through our lives so that we have spontaneity *and* freedom, and our Wild Creature capacities are designed to integrate these into a path we can take.

Summing Up

We know from long human experience that sometimes people can break out of what is keeping them from being happy and free. They can change and grow.

But for every person who breaks free, a dozen others stay caught in old patterns, unable to find a way out. Guilt, frustration, envy, resentment and self-doubt are just a few of the hundreds of words we have for being caught up in our left-hemisphere thinking.

No animal would ever get caught like this. When we use the methods of Wild Creature Mind, it opens a portal between our left and right brains and they come up with answers. A new, wider sense prevails. It can be an exhilarating and liberating moment. And we don't have to leave it to chance.

Often in life, we don't know what is really troubling us. But our Wild Creature does. The job of our right hemisphere is to remember and make sense of things. It knows the path to healing, back into the light.

Chapter 10

Children and Wild Creature Mind

In 1976, I sat in an empty classroom in a Hobart primary school, with a small boy and a box of toys and paints. I was completing research for my Honours dissertation into preventive mental health with children, comparing different ways to help kids who were showing 'risk behaviours'. My group testing of the second-grade classes had identified eight or nine kids, mostly boys, who were seen by the other children as angry, loners or otherwise not quite integrated socially. So we were trialling different forms of intervention, especially a group program for strengthening emotional intelligence called the Human Development Program. It was a beautifully simple format – a twenty-minute small group discussion held every day for six weeks. I would run this myself and see if it made a difference. (It did, but that's another story!)

I had set myself a big task. Most of my fellow students were doing simple lab experiments with volunteer subjects and never left the dark offices of the psych department. I was out in the messy world of real kids. (Cue violins!) Each day, I drove up from the university to the school, gathered the kids and led them in discussions about simple interpersonal skills. How to handle feelings. How to make friends. How to solve conflict peacefully. The program was cleverly designed; it didn't teach or preach, but helped the children explore what worked, and listen to each other on these vital topics that they would rarely otherwise have reflected on. And day by day, the kids learned and grew.

But this one small boy was worrying me. So he received some play therapy sessions too. In the first, I had set out a large sheet of paper, over a metre square, and paints of every colour. He picked up a big brush and began. Within seconds, his face turned into a grimace of concentration and, after a few moments more, almost contorted with anger. Of all the vivid colours, he had chosen the black. His painting quickly took shape – it was of a huge warship taking up almost all of the page, bristling with guns, all shooting streams of bullets. Around it flew tiny aircraft. Each plane had been hit by gunfire, and each one had a small splash of red – the blood of the pilot as he was blown up. Kids carry a lot inside them. The reasons are not hard to imagine. A dad who comes home violently drunk. Parents who put each other down relentlessly. A bullying older sibling. Sexual abuse. We don't know when we look at a classroom full of children what is going on for each of them.

Even for children with great parents and happy lives, childhood is still an *intense* time. There are unavoidable wounds and hurts which are just part of growing up. It's only by coming through these, talking about them, being comforted when overwhelmed, that we learn to *be with* strong emotions, and think our way to resolving them. One of the most valuable things parents do for children is to help them with their inner states, and teach them how to settle from all that has been going on. Parenting books in the past, including my own, have focused on *naming* emotions, helping label them as a way to accept them. But Wild Creature Mind gives an even deeper and therefore more powerful way to help.

SOPHIE AND THE BRAND NEW BIKE

Here is a beautiful example. It's from the Dutch authors Marta Stapert and Erik Verliefte, in their book *Focusing with Children*.

It's Sophie's sixth birthday and she has been given her first two-wheeler bike. Her mum takes her to a park to learn to ride it. Sophie soon gets the knack. In fact, she is way *too* confident, immediately riding off at speed. Seconds later, she crashes on a bend in the path.

When her mum gets there, Sophie is sobbing uncontrollably. Even when they get home, she still hasn't really calmed down. Her mum sits with her.

Mother: Come here I will put a kiss on your knee, then we will drink some lemonade. Maybe the bicycle is a little too big for you after all. Shall I dry your tears? You were going too fast. Did you hear me call out to you? You shouldn't cycle so fast anymore. I will get a bandaid. We will try again tomorrow, you can take it a bit slower.

The difficult thing is that Sophie continues to sob. Then, the mother remembers what she learned in the course on 'focusing with children'. She changes her approach and this helps Sophie discover from within what the essence of the problem really is.

Mother: Shall we listen inside together to hear what happened?

Sophie: Yes.

Mother: You took a really bad fall with your new bicycle. You were doing so well. You dared to go fast. And now you have a scraped knee and it hurts!

Sophie continues to cry and sob.

Yes . . . Yes . . . Yes . . .

Mother: You also have to sob really badly. Can you feel inside where that bad thing is?

Sophie points to her stomach.

Mother: Can you sit with it in a friendly way and ask what it feels like there?

Sophie: It is in my stomach here, really bad (she becomes more quiet and attentive).

Mother: It is in your stomach. How is it there in your stomach?

Sophie: It's all going around (she moves her hands around).

Mother: It just keeps going around inside.

Sophie: . . . just like grabbing hands.

Mother: Just like grabbing hands.

If you keep feeling that, do those grabbing hands have a story to tell you?

Sophie, sobbing loudly now: Yes! Those big girls should not have stood there looking like that . . . I am sure they think I am a stupid little kid.

Mother: You hated that they were standing there looking. They are bigger.

And then you are afraid that they think you are small and stupid.

(There is a pause.)

Mother: Does that feeling have a colour inside? Maybe you can close your eyes for a minute and wait for what comes.

Sophie: Yes. Red is coming and also something black.

Mother: Would you draw and colour it? Your hand will put everything on the sheet of paper. It doesn't have to be beautiful. The feeling will know what it means.

Hesitantly, Sophie starts with dark colours, then the stripes get stronger, the sobbing stops. She scratches with the crayon fiercely, adding more lines, and another colour.

There is a deep sigh. Then there are yellow and orange circles. She looks up at her mother and smiles.

Sophie: It's gone.

There is something truly beautiful about this small episode in a little girl's life, how intimate and fragile it is. How it really helps her to move something – possibly for her whole life – about humiliation. We can't know how this issue came to matter so much to Sophie, but for her, the feelings had nothing to do with the fall, or the hurt knee. Her mum had noticed only concern in the faces of the older girls, and they had not said or done anything to mock. But Sophie felt intense shame, and needed to get through something – perhaps an earlier experience – and it could so easily have been missed.

The words Sophie's mother used are important, and there are two key questions that stand out: 'Can you feel inside where that bad thing is?' Then, after Sophie describes it: 'Can you sit with it in a friendly way and ask it what it feels like there?'

And when Sophie describes it so specifically 'like grabbing hands' her mum knows to not lead or push, but instead to enable the focusing to happen by just staying with the process, and mirroring exactly what her daughter described: 'Just like grabbing hands.'

And perhaps cued by a deep breath or movement in her daughter, she knows it's okay to dive in. 'Do those grabbing hands have a story to tell you?'

And suddenly, they are there. The Shift has happened. Wild Creature Mind and left hemisphere language mind are talking across the void, and she knows what has upset her.

It's a big and painful feeling, this humiliation. As we said, who knows where it comes from? But her mum now turns to the ever-handy paper and crayons or paint, and it can be dealt with by 'externalising' the pain onto paper. Even without the painting, Sophie was already in a better place, but the artwork helps to complete the healing. We can realistically hope that this very specific hurt is not going to occur again in Sophie's life, or if it does, that she will be able to move out of it with more ease.

Every parent will identify with the wild casting about that Sophie's mum did at first; kissing it better, distracting with lemonade, being logical and finally, in exasperation, blaming Sophie for going too fast and not listening! It's a spiral we've all gone down. And then she remembers a better way.

Asking about where the bad feeling is, and patiently listening for what it is trying to say (it might take time), are much more helpful ways of talking to a child, and I hope they will become a part of your vocabulary too.

Accepting What We Cannot Change

Can you handle another story? This example has a boy in it, just to be fair! It's about handling the natural griefs of life, which our felt sense can help to make bearable. (I'm not sure if that's an animal pun or not. We do bear up often in our lives, and it works out fine in the end!)

Ravi is eight years old, a sweet-natured boy who adores his older sister, Satya. Despite the four years between them, they have always been the dearest companions. But this morning, getting ready for school, there was a huge blow-up between them. Satya ended up yelling at the top of her lungs to 'stop bugging me!' and stormed off to catch her bus.

Ravi was distraught. He went to his room in tears. His mum gave him a few minutes and then went in to see if she could comfort him. She was worried that he would be late for school, but knew that without some calming down, his day would not go very well.

She sat beside him on the bed. 'How are you going?' she asked gently.

He didn't answer.

'Satya was really loud and mean to you back then. It must have been a surprise?'

'Yes,' Ravi snuffled.

'And now it's left you feeling awful?'

'She hates me!'

'Well, it feels pretty bad to be talked to in that way.'

'I hate her! I don't want to be her brother anymore.'

Okay! 'Can I ask you, Ravi, can you feel the bad feeling in your body?'

'Yes.'

'Where does that bad feeling live right now?'

A pause. Then: 'It's in my throat.'

'Okay, just feel it there. What is it like?'

'It's tight. My whole throat is tight.'

'Okay.' A pause. 'Ravi, what do you think your throat is wanting to say to you?'

He thinks for a bit. 'Mum, remember when we went to Folk Festival? And Satya held my hand and we danced?'

'Yes, it was your birthday.'

'Satya isn't the same, Mum. She doesn't want to play with me anymore.' He starts to cry.

'You're really sad, you wish it was like it used to be with you two, when we first moved here.'

Ravi is sitting up now, leaning into his mum. 'I had better get going to school!'

'Yes, I will help you get going . . .'

When children get upset, it's often hard to know what to do or say.

When I was a kid, parents used to say things like, 'Quit crying or I'll give you something to cry about!' Still today, we try to distract children, or reason with them or try and talk them out of feeling bad.

Ravi's Wild Creature Mind guides him to the answer. Ravi isn't angry at his sister, really; he is grieving that she is growing up and not his little friend like she used to be. Life has sadness built in sometimes, and all we can do is be there for our kids as they suffer through that.

Ravi has come a long way in the three or four minutes they spent. He now knows something new, that bugging his sister won't turn back the clock, but they can still be friends in a growing way as she enters puberty and lives more in the world of her girlfriends.

Ravi's mum might have a word with Satya to not forget her little brother, and still have time with him, but she won't force her to stay a child. She too knows her daughter is growing up.

Summing Up

Grief is big, especially in childhoods when our hearts are so open, and so tender. We want to keep their hearts open, in a world that works endlessly to close them down. It's a great paradox that if we can feel sorrow fully, then we can become stronger than if we tough it out. When grief large or small visits us, we need other people to help us bear it, but it's entirely manageable, it won't kill us. Wild Creatures are hardy things.

Teaching your children about their Wild Creature Mind, and its signals, is probably the most powerful parenting tool there is, because it gives the power back to them. They can have it forever, long after we are gone. Its power to warn them, to comfort them, and to make them able to self-nurture – all are aspects of this understanding, that 'there is an animal inside you and it is your friend'.

I wish I had my time again with that small boy in his Hobart primary school. And been able to ask him where in his body he felt all that emotion. It might have led to some answers.

GROWING OUR BABIES' WILD CREATURE MINDS

While we've featured Iain McGilchrist as the lead figure in brain hemisphere research, an equally world-renowned expert called Allan Schore, has broken new ground in *how our right hemisphere comes to be*. This understanding dispels any leftover ideas about 'instinct' or 'irrational' aspects of Wild Creature Mind.

Schore writes that between six and twelve months of age, a baby's right hemisphere dramatically increases in size. It grows not just from the passage of time, like a cabbage in the garden, but is actually *built*, through playful and tender interaction with a responsive and relatively happy carer, usually the mum. (Though a dad or grandparent might take this place.) This relationship needs to be close and continuous, but doesn't have to be perfect, in fact it's the stumbles and upsets, once restored, which actually build resilience. The experience of being loved builds pathways between the infant's developing right cortex, and the deep-down places in the right brainstem and right amygdala. These are the places where fear, vigilance and alarm are often set off by the natural events of babyhood – waking in the dark, sudden noises, getting hungry, and so on. It isn't so much what the mother says, or even does, but through unconscious communication from her own Wild Creature Mind. A baby is wired to read a mother's cues in her face, breathing, posture and touch, and enter a kind of dance which builds a greater and greater sense of personhood.

Babies get upset, and we soothe them, in quite elaborate and mostly intuitive ways – like using a high-pitched voice which babies hear very well, mimicking their upset, but then dropping our pitch, making eye contact, smiling, showing concern in frowning back at their frowns, a rather amazing dance which almost all parents do if they are sufficiently relaxed and available. And, of course, if they have seen the same done as they were growing up.

This is not just charming tenderness, but a rock-solid necessity for training a little person's brain to manage and self-soothe its intense feelings. And one more important thing: To experience *a sense of self* – that I am here, I matter, I have impact on others. When I 'find myself in times of trouble', other people come to me! This sense of self is automatically present in someone raised with kindness. But many humans are not raised in a natural- or animal-like way. Poverty, stress, a culture of distance from our children, abuse and war, can all intervene.

Violence, and other controlling behaviour, is an immense problem. But so is suicide, which kills 700,000 people a year worldwide, more than all wars or disasters combined. Schore is convinced that a propensity for violence, and for suicide, are caused by failure to properly develop our right hemisphere. When people do really awful things, to themselves, or to others, then this is almost certainly because there is some breakdown in this deep, unconscious sense of self, so this creates panic, wildly fluctuating heartbeat, blood pressure and respiration, and either escalation or shutdown of body awareness. To be able to take your own life, or be violent to someone else, requires a shocking amount of disintegration on the inside. People who have taken their own lives show evidence in their bloodstreams of wildly diverging serotonin levels. They often have numbed themselves completely from their bodies, too frightened of what they are feeling, and as a result their thinking collapses, not believing anyone cares or thinks they are worth saving. They discount both their own value, and the value of others around them.

If you or someone you know are going through this, please see the Getting Help box on page 85. Helping to prevent this imbalance, or treat it in someone whose childhood just didn't provide the basic ingredients is a huge thing. It takes a caring other person, with as much presence and commitment and willingness to journey into the distress of a full-sized adult, and use their own reserves of love and calm and kindness to navigate them through.

I believe this can be done though, and if a person has managed to stay alive to this point, the right ingredients are there and can be knitted together through solid and honest care, by the provision of what was missing in those babyhood days. It's a big job to soothe all the pain in the world, but the danger of not doing so is worse.

At least now we know what works, and can stop wandering in circles in our thinking about violence, suicide, war and greed. We know what causes them all. We know that it is love which grows the brain, and brings us back to choosing life.

(A great short intro can be viewed on YouTube at 'Dr. Allan Schore on key factors in treating suicidal individuals' or on his website, psychalive.org.)

Teaching your children about their Wild Creature Mind, and its signals, is probably the most powerful parenting tool there is, because it gives the power back to them. They can have it forever, long after we are gone. Its power to warn them, to comfort them, and to make them able to self-nurture – all are aspects of this understanding, that 'there is an animal inside you and it is your friend'.

Chapter 11

When a Feeling Just Won't Shift

Hopefully by now, dear reader, you have been experimenting with Wild Creature methods – to get back to sleep, to know what is right for you, to help heal tough memories when they arise. And just in your daily life so that you are more alive and in tune with the richness of your senses. So it's time to look at what is going on when you still get stuck.

Have you ever had bad feelings that just stick around forever? Months, or even years? Perhaps big feelings, a hurt perhaps, that really affects your relationship with someone. Or a feeling that goes back for years, and seems almost to colour your whole life? When that happens, it's likely that your Wild Creature Mind is shouting at you and you are not paying attention. You are focused on the wrong thing, but you just don't know it.

In September 2022, a young woman wrote to *Guardian* advice columnist Eleanor Gordon–Smith with an interesting, yet relatable question. Gordon–Smith is an ethicist, and an impressive and unusual person, with a focus on figuring out logically, in a murky world, what is right and wrong. She is also good with emotions, as you will soon see:

Dear Eleanor
After years of trying to be the good daughter, I'm finally feeling really angry about my father's affair when I was just a toddler. The woman became my

stepmother and I've always tried to be amenable and just move on.

Now I've realised I have suppressed this hatred for a woman who set out to break up my parents' marriage. How do I have a relationship with my dad if I don't want anything to do with his current wife?

Those two short paragraphs say so much, don't they? It's interesting to think, before we look at Eleanor's response, about what you can glean from this brief summary of a complex situation. So get your detective hat on, and let's go.

1. This goes *way* back. Sally (let's call her that) was first impacted by this affair several decades ago, when she was just a toddler.
2. She lived through the experience of the subsequent marriage break-up. Most likely she had some shared access throughout her formative years, but probably was mostly with her mum, and witnessed her mum dealing with the infidelity and loss of her marriage over that time.
3. Sally spent all those years being a 'nice girl' (and you really feel for her, as she must have decided only this would keep her father's love).
4. She has suddenly realised that she is furious with her stepmum. But she is worried about giving voice to it and risking losing her good relationship with her dad.

You don't need to be Inspector Vera Stanhope to be asking the elephant-in-the-room question here: *how come she isn't angry at her dad?* Men, unless I am badly mistaken, do have an actual active role in whether or not they have an affair. And Eleanor, bless her, is onto this too. But not by the direct route.

Eleanor does something that distinguishes good columnists – she goes wide and offers lots of possible handles on this. (A face-to-face therapist would have a lot more to go on, but on the basis of an anonymous letter, you have to take a few stabs.)

Eleanor writes: There's this line that the half-life of love is forever. I think it can be true for certain kinds of anger, too: with enough time we can make peace with whatever happened to make us so angry, but the feeling itself smoulders to a glow that just keeps pulsing on and on.

Some people think this kind of lingering anger only hurts, and our goal should be to get rid of it. I disagree: I think the emotion of anger can be a way of insisting to ourselves that what happened matters – after everything else has moved on, after new trees have grown tall in the place where we were hurt, the fact of our continued anger can be a memorial to the moral truth of what happened.

181

I am not sure if I follow the first paragraph – and the metaphors get a bit tangled, lovely though they are. The 'tall trees' have grown on pretty boggy ground, and may be about to blow over in the first strong gale. But we agree where it matters – Sally's anger comes from a palpable, life-changing hurt, to her mother and herself. Yet she only recently realised that she felt it. Here is a person very good at suppressing her emotions, and her Wild Creature Mind has been missing in action for almost her whole life. It's all very English! However, that creature is starting to poke its head up.

Eleanor continues:

> But if we're going to choose to live with anger instead of trying to extinguish it fully, we need to be sure we can control it. There is a world of difference between consistently and evenly judging that someone does not yet deserve our forgiveness, and being randomly pulled backwards by the hair into painful memories from years ago.

This part is wonderful. When all is said and done, you have to be a bit surgical about hanging on to old feelings. Twenty-something years ago, someone was willing to be party to the destruction of a family unit, and a child might reasonably feel absolute rage at that. Yet with the passage of time, compassion for the couple and just plain experience of life might abate the intensity. Being an adult might make it less easy to be judgemental. Neither Sally, nor us the readers, really know the inside of things, and it's doubtless more complex than what we can see. It's still a betrayal and a theft, though. It would help if someone asked for forgiveness, and heard the child anguish inside Sally.

Eleanor says some things along these lines, and recalls a schoolfriend who also lost her dad to an affair. She gives a quote from the heart from that schoolfriend, in that brilliant way young people can cut to the quick: 'I'm just angry he thought his happiness was worth every-one else's.'

Then at last, Eleanor gets where we all want her to. She has quietly snuck up on what must be a very confronting and difficult thing for Sally to take on board.

If expressing your feelings about your stepmother doesn't quite lance the boil, *I think it's worth asking if you're angry with your father, too.* Sometimes anger sticks around because there's something else it hasn't said, like a poltergeist keeping you up at night until you can figure out its unfinished business. Perhaps some of this anger is for him.

Instead of freighting all your anger on her and maintaining contact with only him, it might be help-ful, long-term, to grapple with the pain that they

183

represent to you together. Try not to worry that this will mean causing a stir – if they've made it this far in the relationship without recrimination, there's likely a small part of them that's waiting for that shoe to drop.

Anger that keeps burning can do an important job for us in insisting that we matter – the trick is to make sure it casts light and not just heat.

This is great stuff. You can see why the *Guardian* editors chose Eleanor for this job!

Here again is the pivotal line for our purposes.

Sometimes anger sticks around because there's something else it hasn't said, like a poltergeist keeping you up at night until you can figure out its unfinished business.

For poltergeist, substitute Wild Creature Mind. It won't let go, because *we just haven't listened*.

Sally's childhood was fraught. Her father was unfaithful possibly before she was even born. She grew up in a family with a wounded mum, and somehow did not even notice how furious she was with her stepmum, let alone her dad. Her Wild Creature must have felt like an animal trapped in a cellar for over twenty years; thank God it's finally seeing the sunlight!

This whole story so beautifully demonstrates how our body holds our secrets, waiting until we finally listen. Will Sally finally discover her fury at her dad? That's certainly what Eleanor is encouraging. Probably Wild Creature methods might help. In fact, you can't help wishing she had received this help when she was about five. (And 'Sally', if you are reading this, then I and our readers are so grateful for your openness about this struggle, and hope you are now in a really good place.)

Anger will stick around *until we get what it is trying to tell us.* You can love someone, and still be utterly furious, betrayed and devastated by their actions. *How they respond when we let them know this* is the point. Do they cleave to their selfishness, or stand (wo)manfully in the shame they now realise they deserve? Even the right choices sometimes hurt other people, and if they matter to us, then we have to own that. Owning it is the path to being forgiven.

Their willingness to be accountable will tell you whether to keep loving them. You won't have to decide; your Wild Creature self will know. And each day, that will unfold. We all deserve accountability in the people we entrust with our love.

Focusing on the signals in our bodies works so well because this approach doesn't try to tell you what to feel. It allows the process to happen, so that we know ourselves and can figure out what action feels right, and have both sides of the question live in our consciousness: our left brain contributes moral clarity ('it's wrong to deceive, it's wrong to cause needless harm') and our right brain manages the nuanced navigation that is needed to merge our own needs and those of those we care about into a decent, honourable way forwards.

The lesson for everyone? Don't treat forgiveness as a kind of ethical task you must perform. Don't 'fake it till you make it'. Forgiveness is a deep road that has to be travelled. It can't be just wished into existence.

Summing Up

One of the real superpowers of Wild Creature Mind is it basically forgets nothing. It is wired very closely to the limbic system and especially the hippocampus library of memories which our left brain does not have a library card for. So when we are stuck in a bad place, sometimes we have to sit with it and pay really close attention to the felt sensations that go with it. Think 'step-mother/father/infidelity/ongoing relationship' (insert your own stuck situation here!) and then notice what felt sense that stirs inside you. As we search for words to describe it, we create a little neural bridge – a left brain/right brain peace treaty, fragile but hopeful – and across that bridge new thoughts will begin to flow. We discover that the way we have framed things is not the only way. That there are secrets we have been keeping from ourselves. We gain insights that would make a Jungian therapist do a happy dance. We are shining lights in our own darkness, and it's really quite a nice place. Our unconscious, to use that old language for the right hemisphere, is a renovator's dream!

WILD CREATURE ETHICS

Most of us have always believed that ethics are a rational thing. That as we get more mature, we gradually learn the difference between right and wrong. That is partly true, but the ethics researcher Professor Jonathan Haidt of NYU makes a compelling case (in his book *The Righteous Mind*) that morality originates intuitively; in other words, from our Wild Creature Mind. He identified five moral senses which are fundamental to all human cultures (and from some studies, also in chimpanzees). In other words, they are biologically based.

These are:

1. To care and not to harm.
2. To be fair and not to cheat.
3. To be loyal and not to betray.
4. To respect authority versus to subvert authority.
5. To treat life as sacred, versus to commit degradation of living things.

Interestingly, most of us today would query the fourth one, which probably only applied in a clan-based forager society and has somewhat gone off the rails. When those in authority break all the other principles (think of the Boris Johnson government) then clearly subversion is almost a duty! But for the other four, caring, fairness, loyalty and respecting the sacredness of life – we just know in our gut that these matter. The reasoning why they help comes later, and helps them along. But they are based in deep instinctual animal good sense.

It's important to say that we are not arguing that we should always follow our feelings in choosing how to act. Every day in the world hideous violations of those ethics take place by people just doing what they feel. In Konrad Lorenz's work on wolves, he found that there is a complex interaction between aggression – a wolf angered by another wolf's intrusion or challenging of territory or status – and the inhibitory instinct. That if a wolf rolls on its back and submits, the aggressor wolf ceases to attack, and can be seen somewhat struggling between both urges. Wolves are programmed not to take the life of another wolf who is surrendering; it would be bad for the species if wolves killed other wolves. In a human being, we teach our toddlers not to hit or hurt, but this is most successful when it builds on an inbuilt kindness/empathy circuit in their brain. (A toddler can hit another in a playgroup, and within seconds be distressed at the tears they have created!)

Suffice it to say that Wild Creature Mind has ethical foundations, and in combination with left-hemisphere learning about right and wrong, and if we are raised with kindness so that we do not lose the basic sense of connection to others, then we will most often have a 'felt sense' for doing the right thing. We are not an ethical being at war with an evil nature, as the Church taught for two thousand years (despite its founder teaching non-judgementalness). We are better than that.

Chapter 12

Tremoring

For many years, I could sleep like a log, on almost any surface and in any conditions. I've slept on hillsides between Melbourne and Sydney when it was too foggy to hitch the next ride. In a bus, crossing West Bengal with a friend's child asleep on my knee, interrupted only by a brief hijacking by Naxalite rebels. All through the child-rearing years, no problem falling asleep; the only problem was staying awake! It was my superpower. But a couple of years ago, that ability seemed to desert me.

Just like James (and probably many people reading this book), I began to have nights of racing anxiety. There were reasons to worry – midway among three generations of extended family with its fair share of health and practical worries. But that was not a new thing; somehow, in my mid-sixties, I had just lost my resilience.

I was not alone. About ten per cent of adults have insomnia at any one time, and 30 per cent will experience it in their lifetime, and it's clearly worse in times of stress or worry. These wasted nighttime hours were making me lose energy in the daytime, and so were really important to address.

Luckily, I was researching and learning about the focusing sequence. It was a no-brainer to apply this to myself. On one especially bad night, I said, 'Right, here goes,' and gently rallied my brain. I sent my awareness into my body and located where my greatest discomfort was. Not hard to find – my heart was racing quite fast and my chest very tight. I acknowledged it, made it welcome and tried to soften my chest to give it more room. All at once, and to my great surprise, a single convulsive shudder, like an electric shock, ran through my body. An involuntary movement large enough to rattle the headboard. 'Hmm,' I thought, 'that was interesting!'

The Cambridge dictionary defines shudder as 'to shake suddenly with very small movements because of a very unpleasant thought or feeling'. Robert Bly wrote 'never trust a man who cannot shudder'. It's a natural reaction to being appalled or horrified. Clearly then our body is doing something, and therefore our mind is too.

Many years earlier, I had come across the therapy method of tremoring, a way to induce physical shuddering that seems to release a great deal of the held-in tension which some people hold in their bodies. In the 1980s, I was a Churchill Fellow, and travelled the world to learn from some of the best therapists of that time. I had witnessed and participated in breathing and body therapies which involved putting oneself into a 'stress position' – for example, standing like a karate student, with legs apart and knees bent, and relaxing all over. Within about 30 seconds, the muscles in one's legs would start to tremble, and a whole-body trembling would take over. It was very releasing to do these exercises, like a one-hour workout in 60 seconds, requiring little effort but exercising every muscle in the body. From this I learned that *bodies do this*.

So I was not perturbed when in a therapy group I was leading, in the 1980s, a young woman began to shake violently all over while talking about her life. Melanie had been a patient of mine, and (without going into specifics) had made an impressive and courageous journey, after a horrendous early life. Now, in the group, which was a friendly and supportive one, she had been talking about some present-day difficulties, and simply began to tremble all over. It wasn't distressing to her, or even overwhelming, she was able to comment wryly along the lines of 'wow, here I go' and went with it. She keeled over from her sitting position on the floor and was soon bucking and shaking, her arms and legs kicking, almost like a seizure, but was able to comment from time to time to reassure us that it was okay. We simply sat and encouraged her to feel safe and 'let it come', being careful, given her history, not to go too close or touch her.

After about a minute (which is quite a long time), the trembling subsided and I could see she was breathing easily. As much for the group's reassurance (since I was pretty sure of the answer) I asked if she was okay, and she murmured yes. Her husband came over from his position on the other side of the room, and sat beside her and she nestled into him. She looked bright and alive, if somewhat exhausted. And we went on to the next person.

Some years later I had the same experience myself, sitting with some therapist friends, after an intense afternoon's training. We were just getting ready to head for home, but I and some others were still seated on the floor. I felt an upwelling of emotion and, perhaps on some level sensing that it was as safe an environment as I could ever have, I spontaneously just let the feelings come. And was in just a few seconds convulsed with sobbing and rolled onto my side curled up in a ball like a little child. My friends were unfazed, sat close and held me lightly – intuiting that this was what would help, being alert in case I did not want that – and feeling the care in that holding, I went even deeper for two or three minutes, shaking, gasping and sobbing, while they kept strong hands on my back and head. (My trauma as a child was more about not being touched or held, and so people being close was very important, the complete opposite of Melanie.) I should say that none of this was distressing, I could watch it all objectively, I felt nothing more than mild surprise, but mostly pure release and an acknowledgement that I had probably been under more stress than I had realised, possibly for many years. And it was now time to let it go.

Decades later, in 2021 when I had that single shudder, it all came back to me. The next morning I telephoned a friend who I knew was interested in the phenomenon of 'tremoring'. I was keen to learn more from someone who knew the science. Richmond Heath is a physiotherapist, and is active in men's mental health in Australia. During the pandemic, Richmond decided to be of service by creating an online course in how to tremor, safely and well. I signed right up. It was to change my life.

TRE

Tension/Trauma Release Exercises (TRE) is a system that uses a natural mechanism which all animals possess to downregulate their nervous system and let go of tension, physical and mental.

When a sudden adrenaline rush is triggered by a dramatic event, or even just a threat, or perception, then our sympathetic nervous system goes into overdrive because we may well need to get active! To run, fight, freeze or otherwise muster extraordinary resources to survive. But many events are 'near misses' or take a different tack, so that we are left in an upregulated state – 'all stressed up with nowhere to go'. Almost every modern life challenge – a near miss in a car while driving to work, making a presentation or speech, or getting up the courage to ask someone out – leaves an overshoot of adrenaline coursing through our bodies when it's over. The biological method that mammals naturally use to get back to normal is to discharge through shaking and shuddering, so that the muscles can burn off that adrenaline and let the tension go.

In our Western, stiff-upper-lip approach to life, we misinterpreted 'getting the shakes' as a sign of something going wrong. It's not – shuddering and shaking is a good thing. We even get the shakes when happy or excited – winning the lottery is a good example. Millions of soldiers and first responders as well as anyone facing a challenge – speaking at a wedding, proposing marriage, being on a first date, accepting an Oscar – just your usual life events LOL, might experience the shakes.

It's very important (see box on page 204) for anyone in a profession with inbuilt stress to know that the shakes means something is going *right* with their body. This is our body's own way of *preventing* PTSD.

TRE is a set of extremely simple exercises which evoke this natural mild trembling in order to *get that down-regulation restarted*. It helps the body let go of holding patterns in muscles and nerves which might even be decades old. It's wonderful stuff.

Richmond points out in his course, and has videos to illustrate, that animals all shudder routinely. A dog left tied up outside the supermarket while its owner shops has a great urge in its legs to run inside after them, which it cannot do. Its thighs shake and twitch for a while, then it settles down. It's pure physiology, letting an urge and its associated adrenaline discharge harmlessly so self-regulation can be restored. A prey animal like a deer or rabbit does this after escaping a predator (we have to assume it's terrifying to be almost brought down by a cheetah or wolf) and these animals *seem to suffer no ill effects at all.*

Safe in their burrow, or a thicket hidden away, they shake it all out.

EXERCISE: HOW TO TREMOR

A great thing about TRE is that you can do it lying down, on your bed, for example. (Almost everyone I know who uses TRE does it to be able to get to sleep.)

The trick is to induce some fatigue in a muscle group so that it begins to tremor. You can do this most easily with a 'stress position'. The safest and easiest stress position is lying on one's back on a rug or mat, with a pillow under your head if needed. Bending one's knees, feet touching alongside each other, open the knees and thighs in a butterfly kind of way.

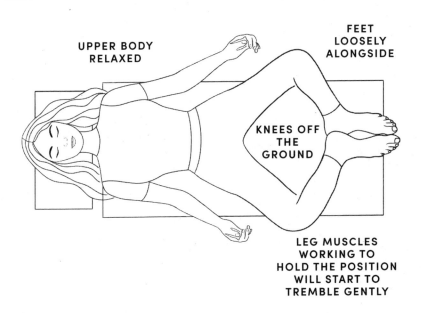

UPPER BODY
RELAXED

FEET
LOOSELY
ALONGSIDE

KNEES OFF
THE
GROUND

LEG MUSCLES
WORKING TO
HOLD THE POSITION
WILL START TO
TREMBLE GENTLY

Let your knees fall all the way out to the sides, where the natural stretchiness of your tendons will stop them. Then lift them back up a little bit, just an inch or two, and hold them there. If you keep your legs reasonably relaxed while doing this, at some point (usually in less than 30 seconds), they will start to shake. This is simply from fatigue in the muscles holding an unusual position against gravity.

Now, if you stay relaxed (and there is a slight knack to this – a kind of 'allowing'), then the shaking in your legs will usually start to increase, and often spread up into your pelvis and torso, and even as far up as your shoulders, arms and head. You are soon 'going off', with your whole body shaking and trembling. (Those of a

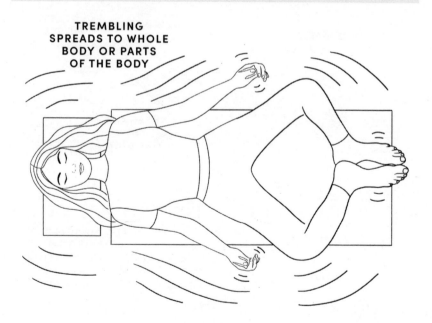

TREMBLING
SPREADS TO WHOLE
BODY OR PARTS
OF THE BODY

sensuous nature will be aware of an orgasm-like quality to this, and yes, I am sure many of the same muscles are involved, and certainly the experience is pleasant, and just a little cosmic. It might be a good idea to explain to your partner or housemate what you are doing to avoid misunderstanding!)

You can stop the shuddering at any time if you find it unsettling, and just feel the ground under you and look about a little while lying still. But if you are willing to just let it keep happening, you might find that it's pleasant and releasing to just go with until it naturally stops. You may feel a wish to roll onto one side or curl up into a ball and tremor in this position, or to just go still. Trust your body to know what it wants to do and, if unsure, just experiment a little.

When you are first learning how to tremor, it's important to feel safe and relaxed so you don't get overwhelmed and can let your body move freely, so if you start to notice bracing or holding anywhere in your body or even in your breath, slide your legs out straight and have a rest until you are fully relaxed and ready to start again.

It's quite likely that your breathing might also take on a convulsive, panting nature and if there are emotions close to the surface, they will very likely emerge. You might find yourself sobbing or moaning. Some people simply laugh. Ultimately, your body will move and tremor however it needs to, so you don't need to compare your tremors to anyone else's or expect a specific result.

Richmond's online course www.trecourse.com guides you through all of this. Using the TRE model (first developed by Dr David Bercelli), the course is very conservative and careful in pacing the experience and helping you rebalance when it's over, and absorb the benefits fully. Many of the benefits really 'land' after the tremoring itself passes and you integrate the new looseness and freedom in your muscles and nerves.

Memories Reintegrating

Tremoring is a Wild Creature activity, and it might well feed memories forwards as it resolves old experiences. On the second session of the online course, I felt an urge to roll over into a curved shape like a sleeping child. Odd sensations surrounded my mouth and lips, and then I remembered something.

Many children of my vintage – born in the 1950s – had their tonsils removed as a routine thing. Tonsils are a kind of lymph node at the side of the throat, and in those days were believed to harbour TB and other diseases. Millions of kids had their tonsils out, and when I was four, our family doctor thought I should too.

Off to hospital I went. I spent the first night in the large ward with 50 or so other kids. Then, early the next afternoon, a nurse brought what I only years later learned was a pre-med – a drink with a strong sedative. This was so I would be dreamy and unfussed when wheeled into theatre and clamped with a gas mask to knock me out properly.

I just thought it was cordial! I put it to my lips, but mid-gulp, suddenly noticed the colour – it was blue! Combined with the odd taste, I did what any sensible four-year-old would – I spat it out all over the bedsheets. Furious with me, the nurse was not about to give me another cup, but instead stormed off to find clean sheets. I doubt if she told the operating team. Ten minutes later, I was fighting tooth-and-nail in the theatre as a team of nurses tried to clamp me with a gas mask, the icy-cold gas pushing its way into my lungs. My last memory was of one of the nurses who I had taken a shine to (she was young, tall and dark-haired like my mum). She was one of the assassins who were trying to do me in!

I forgot about this for about 60 years, but there, lying on my living room rug, Heath's reassuring voice playing on my laptop, I could actually feel the cold rubber on my face. I seemed to be all shuddered out, so I just marvelled at the magic of the mind and body, and lay there peacefully for a while, tingling all over.

Tremoring has become part of my life now. Perhaps once a week I do the whole procedure on purpose, just when I feel a bit tense and not properly in my body. It's like a reset on any accumulated tension, and perhaps even a deeper clean as bits of my life get tidied away on a neural level. But the main change is more involuntary and natural, and very helpful. Often several times a day, usually when nobody is around, my thoughts are triggered by something, an upsetting news story or just something I am thinking about, and zap, there it goes. A single shudder. Sometimes a second one following on. And it always leaves me more peaceful.

It's something our Wild Creature Mind does to keep us well.

WHAT EVERY FIRST RESPONDER NEEDS TO KNOW ABOUT ADRENALINE: BY RICHMOND HEATH

By its very nature frontline work is a high-adrenaline environment – from extreme adrenaline surges lasting up to an hour after critical incidents, to the slow-burn levels required for trained hypervigilance, managing conflict and high intensity stress.

The problem most first responders face is generally not a lack of adrenaline (although that can occur during burnout) but the inability to reduce adrenaline levels when it is time to switch off, unwind and sleep peacefully after their shifts.

What every first responder needs to know about adrenaline is that it does not 'cause' their body to shake or tremble as commonly thought, as these involuntary movements play no part in the fight or flight response whatsoever.

Instead, these spontaneous movements are a *natural recovery response*, dissipating adrenaline by 'using it up' in an energy-efficient way to restore circulating levels to homeostatic balance.

Currently, most first responders misunderstand this shaking response as being 'caused' by adrenaline and see it as a 'symptom' of shock, anxiety or even PTSD. As it is also commonly stigmatised as a sign of weakness or lack of control, they therefore generally attempt to suppress it – both in themselves and the people they are assisting.

Inadvertently, the inhibition of this resilience reflex results in incomplete recovery and elevated adrenaline levels, leading to chronic arousal and neuromuscular tension as insidious factors in the progressive loss of wellbeing and resilience currently experienced across the frontline career.

Conversely, this recovery reflex can be deliberately invoked in a safe and controlled way using the body-based self-care technique TRE – providing first responders with an 'active recovery' technique to help them switch off, regulate their adrenaline levels and literally shake off the stress and trauma they are currently accumulating across their careers.

How Your Body Remembers

Peter Levine is an unassuming chap, about 60, grey-haired with twinkling eyes. He is a psychologist who has specialised in stress for most of his career, working with first responders, soldiers and crime victims. But it was a dramatic personal experience which gave him the most penetrating understanding of how our bodies work to get through intense experiences . . .

Peter is walking one afternoon near his home, on his way to the birthday party of an elderly friend. He goes onto a pedestrian crossing, and *bang!* – suddenly everything goes black. He 'comes to' to find that he is on his back lying on the road, unable to move his body and struggling to breathe. A crowd of people have rushed over and are hovering over him ('like carnivorous ravens' is how he remembers it). His eyes dart around and the 'what has happened?' becomes clear: the grille of a car looms nearby, and a horror-struck teenage girl bursts out from the driver's side.

There is little time to think. A man's voice is shouting at him, and as he goes to turn towards the voice, it shouts again. 'Don't move your head!' The man announces loudly that he is an off-duty paramedic, and at the same moment, he awkwardly pinions Peter's head. The well-intentioned but totally insensitive man is firing questions rapidly: 'What is your name?', 'What is today's date?' but Peter can't get his brain to connect with his mouth. The voice and manner feel so hostile that he is terrified. Finally, he manages to utter, 'Please back off' and 'I won't move my head'. It must be convincing, as the man backs off.

Several moments pass. An ambulance has been called. Peter just lies there. Then, something brilliant happens.

Peter sees a woman quietly come forward, and she sits down beside him. She tells him, 'I'm a doctor, a pediatrician. Can I help?'

Peter responds, 'Please, just stay with me.'

She smiles and takes his hand, and he squeezes hers in response. And finally, with this bond established, his nervous system starts to work to resolve what has happened. His body gives a big shudder, and he takes his first proper deep breath. Tears stream from his eyes. He remembers that a couple of minutes ago, he was happily just going to see his friend and feels a wave of feelings – regret, fear ('Am I paralysed?'), sorrow ('How could this happen?'). Meanwhile, his body continues its soft trembling.

The doctor has kept her word; she is still there, watching him. He can smell her perfume. And then comes the next wave – a flood of tingling in his body, then furious rage ('How could that stupid kid hit me on a pedestrian crossing . . .'). But this passes, and again, he just looks at the doctor's face; she is calm and he calms down by seeing that.

Then, with sirens blaring, the ambulance arrives. The ambulance team are adrenalised, concerned for him. They announce that they will take him to a larger hospital because of his injuries. But Peter is more alert now – he goes inside himself and discovers 'an intense, uncomfortable buzzing throughout my body'. Then it starts to localise. (This is a pattern, dear reader, you will come to know well whenever you attend properly to distress inside you. It almost always begins to crystalise in one location.)

His left arm has a strong sensation of wanting to rise up and he can feel his hand rotate, and as he notices that – *bang* – the memory comes to him, of hitting the bonnet of the car, seeing the girl's face through the windscreen, and his arm and hand protecting his head. His memory is now filling in the gaps in what happened, the muscle memory of the action his body took automatically.

He rests for a while as the ambulance continues its journey, then another phase happens. Strong tension comes into his upper back this time, an urge to extend his *right* arm – and the image of the black bitumen of the road coming towards him, the actual sound of his hand hitting it to reduce the impact, and he feels the actual pain of it in his hand now.

In short, Peter's body is completing what it needed to do to recover. By the time they reach the hospital, Peter and the first responder are discussing his pulse rate, which has now lowered from 170 to just 74. She tells him about other road trauma victims she has seen, and that the shaking his body was doing is usually regarded with dismay, and valium injected. But he is convincing her that the shaking is what is needed.

He will suffer no PTSD symptoms from this incident, which was very much on the cards, a fact he attributes to getting support and letting his body do its job.

By focusing and listening to his Wild Creature signals, he invites the completion of his self-protective responses. A mixture of muscle discharge, emotional flashes and memories knitting back together.

To recap the steps that Peter went through automatically, as his Wild Creature Mind took over and carried him through:

- Emotional support.
- Shaking and crying.
- Reorientation, regret, figuring out what happened.
- Fury at the cause of such trauma, mental and physical.
- Left arm completes the fending action to save his head.
- Right arm completes the action it needed to make to lessen the impact on the road.
- Heart rate regulates.

It's a sequence every human being, from babyhood onwards, hopefully is able to make hundreds of times to heal from small to large affronts to our wellbeing, and which in our modern world is very often interrupted or misunderstood. And so the trauma stays in our bodies to impair our happiness and health.

Peter is clear – the calm presence of others was vital. Just as when we are small, our feelings can be too frightening to feel, but if someone is there with us who is not panicked, we can give in to the floods of emotions and they can do their job of restoring our integrity.

Peter Levine's Somatic Experiencing Therapy is a powerful form of Wild Creature–centred treatment. His book *In An Unspoken Voice* is a great and comprehensive read. He covers many methods to evoke and restore healing processes, and I recommend it to anyone wanting to explore the cutting edge of psychotherapy.

Summing Up

In the compelling words of Bessel van der Kolk, 'the body keeps the score'. Our bodies, if they need to, will keep painful emotions in storage – in muscles, memories and nerves – until we feel safe enough to let go. But if we forget to – or are unable to let go – then we become chronically tense, with disabling symptoms like tight shoulders, constricted throats, stooped heads leading to neck problems and so on.

Animals shake when they have been holding back an impulse, or have come through something scary. We can do the same, and TRE exercises help you get started. Tremoring discharges adrenaline, and lets us (again, in van der Kolk's words) 'feel what we feel, and know what we know'. But you don't need to know where the tension came from to release it.

The benefits are immediate; you just feel a whole lot better.

By going with your animal side in this safe way, you will little by little come to have a body that is relaxed and flexible, with good circulation, and be able to shake off trouble and return to feeling happy and alive.

It's very important for anyone in a profession with inbuilt stress to know that getting the shakes means something is going right *with their body. This is our body's own way of* preventing *PTSD.*

Chapter 13

Things That Go 'Eeek!' in the Night

How to Fix Nightmares and Understand Dreams

Chased by angry bandicoots? Flying like Superman over an ocean of strawberry yoghurt? A tsunami washing away your workplace?

Dreams are mysterious things. They have fascinated us through all of time, and even today continue to attract researchers as we try to understand how they work, and what they do for us.

This research is starting to bear fruit, and a new breed of therapists are stepping up to help people with science-based approaches to 'solving' our dreams. As it turns out, Wild Creature Mind is at the very centre of the action. As usual, it is trying to help us.

The most troubling of dreams, of course, are nightmares, which affect everybody at times, but are much worse in people who have come through bad experiences. We all feel great sympathy for the war veteran or other survivor of terrible events waking in terror thinking they are 'back there'. It's no mistake that we call any bad situation a 'nightmare' – they can be profoundly distressing, and they are definitely an indicator of our mind needing some time and care.

In this chapter, we will look at some tools for defusing nightmares so that they stop upsetting you, and help even the most persistent ones to gradually resolve and leave you in peace. And if you don't have especially bad dreams, you can still learn how to benefit from any dream so as to know yourself better.

It Takes Two Sides to Dream

Recent brain studies around the world have shown that during peaceful, non-dreaming sleep, the two sides of our brain barely talk to each other. But at the onset of dreaming, the two sides suddenly light up like a city coming out of a power cut, in a kind of resonating dance. Our two minds are very busy when we dream; it's clearly some kind of collaboration.

Knowing our Wild Creature side is involved, we can make that same attitude shift which has appeared all through this book. From seeing disturbing symptoms as a problem or malfunction to realising they are 'something in us' just trying to do its job. Nightmares are a curative process in need of support to complete their course. Our aim should not be just to cure bad dreams, but to learn what they are trying to tell us.

Listening to Our Nightmares

Here is a personal instance. Just as I was writing this chapter, I had a dream which left me rather ragged and exhausted on waking up. Most of my dreams are totally random, and I rarely remember them for more than a minute or so after waking – if at all. This is totally fine, they have done their job, which science now believes is to sort and finish leftover emotions and situations from the day before (a kind of nightly spring-cleaning of your brain ready for the next day. And like spring-cleaning, some of us just have a pretty big pile of junk to get rid of!).

The work done by dreams normally happens automatically – without our intervention – unless we want to explore more, by doing things like dream journals. If I was in prison or held hostage, I would probably do this as it would be diverting and possibly quite profound, but like most people today, I am a bit too busy!

But throughout my life, some dreams have recurred with a recognisable theme, over and over again, and woken me up with a thumping heart. For almost 40 years, I had nightmares, perhaps once a month or so, that I was still a university student, getting lost in corridors, late for exams, not understanding the lectures and not able to make friends. These elements would recombine in all kinds of horror scenarios, but the theme was always the same. It's no surprise that I had these dreams, because that is pretty much what it *was* like for me at university. I was a working-class kid, nobody from my school went to that university. I was only sixteen, and had undiagnosed Asperger's syndrome. It was the worst time of my life. (I will pause here for sympathy! Okay, now, on we go.)

What was unsettling though, was that those dreams continued for decades. Even in my fifties, I would wake up shaken and have to remind myself that I eventually did graduate, and I never have to go back to another lecture or sit another exam. (I have talked to many people who have school or university dreams, and think it might indicate some reforms necessary to make universities less discouraging places!) Eventually, I just stopped having these dreams. My body had learned it was safe – I'd survived my education.

This pattern – of gradual fading of a nightmare – is exactly the one that most people go through who have had immeasurably worse trauma than I. Survivors of Auschwitz concentration camp have been studied, and ten per cent had horrific nightmares for the rest of their lives. But the rest found that they lessened, and began to become 'mixed' dreams, with elements of reassurance entering into them. For example, one elderly man still dreamed of being in Auschwitz, but his new, younger wife, who was not a Holocaust victim, would be there with him, and he did not feel afraid; he knew deep down that he would survive.

So his mind brought healing elements into the dream life and made it a bridge from horror to healing.

I learned this story from the outstanding Canadian dream therapist Dr Leslie Ellis. A superb teacher and practitioner in the dreaming field, Leslie lives in British Columbia, Canada. Her excellent writing, and eventually kindness in corresponding with me, was the basis of much of this chapter, and I am very indebted to her. Leslie has built on the work of Eugene Gendlin in using focusing – Wild Creature methods – to take the dream story and use it towards healing our waking lives. Gendlin wrote an excellent book about dreams and developed two major tools. One is to 'look for a helper'; the other is what I call 'going to the opposite'. Let's unpack these.

My university nightmares healed themselves (though if I had met Leslie back in my twenties I might have been saved 30 years of stress. Of course, she wasn't even born then!) But by my fifties, a new nightmare theme had emerged. To understand this, I have to explain that my career has followed an unusual path for a psychologist. From early on, I was very keen to improve the lives of parents and children, and I started to give talks. These talks grew into shows which became my full-time work and I toured for about 30 years all over the world. I loved storytelling, feeling myself and the audience travel from laughter to tears and back again. It was a demanding job, but I never felt more than a useful amount of adrenaline to help me rock through that 90 minutes on stage.

But every couple of months, I would have a nightmare about working with a small therapy group and not being able to secure the right room. It was too big or too noisy or the walls collapsed. People could not hear properly and got distracted. I could not 'hold the space'. We would be double-booked with an interpretive dance group who would not negotiate! The dreams were always about the facilities, something not under my control.

Recently I had one of these dreams, the first in many months. (Sorry for the long digression.) On waking, I went out into the early morning garden to clear my head. And I remembered what Gendlin and Ellis wrote about – to 'look for the helper'.

In many dreams, if not all, there will be a figure, often an animal or a child or a green living thing. They are never a major part in the dream's drama, but are still in the dream for a reason. In my latest nightmare, I had noticed, just quietly in the background, a person I know called Helen. Helen is a very strong and warm woman who had been one of my trainees back in the 1980s and we've stayed friends. She didn't do anything in the dream; she was just there. Which was interesting. Clearly, she was the helper.

Nightmare Method 1 – Using the Helper

Instead of the rather tepid activity of 'insight' – figuring out dreams in theory – or 'interpretation', as the psycho-analysts wasted centuries of time doing, the best way to do dreamwork is to feel down, experientially, into what the key characters are all about. To 'occupy' them in turn.

To use the helper, as you come out of a dream or nightmare, get yourself grounded and back in the waking world. Then, when you figure out which element in the dream might be the helper (it doesn't matter who you choose), use your Wild Creature felt sense to 'go inside' that element. It is a part of your own mind, and if you use focusing methods – observing closely the body sensations that go with that figure – then you will bring it to full life.

As I walked in my garden in the early morning, I gave this a try. I went from picturing Helen to imagining *that I was Helen*; what it would be like to be in her body, with her attitudes and character and resources. How Helen would stand, move and most especially *feel*. Now, an important thing to be clear about here is that this is all *my version* of Helen, not how she might actually feel at all. My mind, in constructing the dream, had noted some qualities I perceive in her and had brought her there specifically to help me get over something. And because she was a product of my mind, I almost instantly could use felt sense to access what she represented. She sprang to life in my body.

My felt sense of 'being Helen' was that her body feels absolutely rock solid. Not rigid, but muscular and resolute. Full of energy. Quite prepared to heap scorn where it is merited, or laugh off the craziness of the world and walk away.

It's the very opposite of my timid persona. It feels good to 'be' my imaginary Helen, and so there is a shift. When I go back to myself, her strength is in me too. I am laughing out loud as I go to make myself a breakfast of raw meat. (Not really, but you get the drift!)

Since doing that mental exercise, the 'workshop venue nightmare' has never recurred, but if it did, I would work on it some more using the same methods.

Finding the helper is a wonderful tool to bring in powers and abilities which you actually have, but were missing from your left hemisphere's story of who you are. (You might have to re-read that sentence, there is a lot in there!) Updating that old self-image to the much more resourced person that you are now.

You can see how this makes a dream – especially a recurring one – a real opening to changing who you are in your life in the real world.

Nightmare Method 2 – Going to The Opposite

An even deeper method to use in healing nightmares is one I call 'going to the opposite'. (Gendlin called it 'bias control', but that is a little complex for our purposes.)

Here is an example which Dr Leslie Ellis uses to illustrate this approach:

A man dreams that he is walking up to a cabin in the mountains. His partner, called Sandy, is already in the cabin. Suddenly a man with a knife overtakes him on the trail, running towards the cabin!

It's a short dream but a very potent one. The patient is no fool, he knows that 'everything in a dream is part of us', and he figures out that the man with the knife represents his own anger at his partner. He feels that this is a side of him which is 'resentful, immature and destructive'. He thinks the best thing is to suppress such feelings. But this isn't how dreams work! The dream – like every dream we ever have – is trying to help him be more whole.

Gendlin asks the dreamer to go into his body and feel what it is like to be the knife-wielding man. (To be the opposite of his normal, polite and considerate self.) And then he discovers a surprising thing. The feeling of being inside the knife-carrying man is 'not exactly anger, but more an insistence on being heard'.

223

Gendlin said, 'Sometimes a person is so condemning of the missing part that it seems negative at first . . . freeing it up, letting it live in your body for a minute will let you sense a quality you will like.'

The patient finds to his surprise, this strength feels really comfortable in his body. By going to the opposite, the dreamer is 'trying on' the missing or hidden parts of his true nature, his Wild Creature self, and is able to take those parts that are healthy and helpful on board. What the Jungians call 'eating his shadow'. He becomes more able to stand his ground, be less whiny, less passive aggressive. Not in any way a misogynist, but just real and present. And a far more satisfying partner. And one you can feel safe with.

EXERCISE: PUTTING IT ALL TOGETHER
Here is how you do it.

1. You awaken from a dream, possibly really upset, but at least with an uneasy feeling that it was not a fun experience. The content of the dream might be obvious or quite obscure. All that matters is that you have been left unsettled.
2. Be really clear in your mind that this is not a malfunction. You aren't 'cracking up'; this is your Wild

Creature Mind attempting to get you over a hurdle or piece of trauma, and simply not quite getting there. It is *bringing something to your attention*.

3. Your first job is to re-regulate your upset physiology, to reassure your body that you are safe and okay. You do this by waking up more deliberately – get out of bed, or at least sit up and put on a light, look at your surroundings deliberately. Don't just fall asleep again (you can, but it kind of wastes all you have been through!). If you are really rattled and your heart is racing, practise a couple of deep slow breaths. Breathe longer on the out breaths, and do this until your heartbeat slows, your shoulders drop, your eyes soften.

4. Now, from this distance, have a look at the actual dream. You will find that your distress or difficulty in the dream was caused by *something missing* or some quality or resource being needed, by 'you-in-the-dream'. For example, you had no safe place. Or you were vulnerable to someone larger. You were lost in endless corridors. Or in some other way, you needed *something* in order to feel good and safe in the narrative of the dream.

5. Decide if you can find a helper in the dream. Or if you want to 'go to the opposite'. Now, think of that character or element, and feel your way into the

character using Wild Creature awareness – what felt sense do you have when you picture being that character or element? Follow the usual way – try different words to describe the sensations, and check if those feel right, changing or trying out new words until you find a good fit. Notice how your felt sense changes as you do so, and what comes up in your thoughts as a result.

And that is all you have to do. Your Wild Creature Mind will merge these elements into a whole, little by little, because it's in the nature of the right hemisphere to be whole. You will find yourself less conflicted, less afraid, more unified and strong, little by little. And your dream will have done its job.

AN ANIMAL NEEDS ITS SLEEP!

The natural and timeless pattern for humans was to be awake in the daylight and asleep in the dark. Often we woke for an interval in the middle of the night, and when we lived communally this was a time for quiet chats, making love, telling stories in the semi-darkness round the fire. All animals need sleep; some, like koalas or sloths, do little else! (Researchers think we need an hour of sleep for every two hours of waking, for the brain to tidy up what has happened during the day. Of course, for sloths, that might be – not much!)

But there's a problem. The way we live now has dramatically shortened our sleeping time. Since the 1970s we have reduced our nightly sleeping time by about four hours! Bright lights in our homes, and in the outdoor environment at night, and routine use of alarm clocks both combine, to rob us of sleep and of dreaming time. Because we do our best dreaming just before awakening, using an alarm clock damages and interrupts this vital mental clean-up. It literally steals our dreams. It's like leaving the movies ten minutes before the end of the film!

America's National Sleep Foundation carried out a study that found that more than half of American adults 'needed' an alarm clock to wake up in the morning. More alarmingly, 70 per cent of young adults aged 18–29 did so. In my book *Raising Girls*, Dr Michael Carr-Gregg wrote a section on teenage sleep, which points out that teenagers actually have a time-shifted sleep cycle wired in. Their bodies need this because of the massive brain changes they are undergoing in adolescence. *Teenagers' brains and bodies need to sleep late in the mornings.* Every parent of a teenager sees this – and the dramas it causes. Michael argues that schools should shift their starting times for this age group, and a few brave public schools have been trialling this idea.

Anything we can do to improve sleep conditions will help. Learning to dim or reduce light at night and avoiding screen use for an hour (preferably two) before bedtime are the big first steps we can take. Overbright environments, rather shockingly, are linked with obesity and cancer, as well as depression.

Sleep is a big health issue and it starts in childhood. It's so important to look after our Wild Creature with well-darkened, quiet bedrooms, soft lighting after dinner time and, if possible, allowing yourself to waken naturally. That might take some changes in the big world, but do the best you can. Good sleep will fix a whole lot of your other health issues. It's worth putting it at the top of your list.

Summing Up

Dreams and nightmares are unique collaborations between Wild Creature Mind and thinking mind. If they are too upsetting, or frighten us into waking, then we have to use Wild Creature methods to help them along. Finding the helper and going to the opposite are profound techniques for addressing nightmares especially. These methods use the clues already in the dream as a portal into our bigger self. They help us to enlarge from 'the story we have about who we are' (vulnerable, timid, trapped – which were all once true but no longer are) into a more powerful, safe, healthy and connected self. Dreams are a turbo-boosted way to grow and heal. We'd be crazy not to use them.

During peaceful, non-dreaming sleep, the two sides of our brain barely talk to each other. But at the onset of dreaming, the two sides suddenly light up like a city coming out of a power cut, in a kind of resonating dance. Our two minds are very busy when we dream; it's clearly some kind of collaboration.

Chapter 14

Herd Creatures

Why We Need Each Other to Really be Free

It's one of the most strange and beautiful things I have seen. It was in the documentary *The Secret Life of Elephants*. Two juvenile elephants travelling with their own herd come across the body of another elephant they know from a neighbouring group.

They approach the body cautiously. The younger elephant moves closer and sniffs, not just fleetingly, but for several minutes, almost as if it is hoovering in some kind of scent impressions; as if it is reading a story. Living elephants do this with each other all the time, taking in olfactory signals which can reach back into the history of each other, where they have been, what they have done.

What is most touching is the behaviour of the slightly older elephant. It drapes its own trunk across the shoulders of its younger companion, somehow bracing it or embracing it. We're always warned against attributing human meanings to animal behaviour, but in recent decades, that attitude has begun to change. And I am convinced – it is impossible not to see this as comforting.

Elephants confronted with death show many remarkable behaviours akin to our own grieving, as do the great apes and many other animals and birds. They do not simply 'move on'. It seems important to them to 'process' or, dare we say, 'understand' the fact that this is someone that they cared about who is now gone.

The elephant example is very central to the message of this book in two ways. First, felt sense guides elephants in all that they do. It makes them sociable and caring. Second, the essence of being an elephant is being part of a group. They do life in a team.

We humans are the same. When medical researchers look for causes in everything from heart disease to depression, they identify social supports – friendships, family – as the biggest risk factors of all. Loneliness is the reason that men, who in modern life often have far fewer deep relationships outside the family, are at far higher risk for suicide, violence and so on.

Many of the 'proper human forms' have been lost from the way we live. We live in isolating separate houses fenced off from our neighbours. We separate each day to go to work and school, only having a few hours together at the end of the day. We farm out the care of our babies to strangers and, at the other end of life, we farm out the care of our elderly parents. We have massive working hours, pressured childhoods. I think that if we were to listen to our Wild Creature Minds, they would be in revolt against all of this. The loneliness. The pressure. The hurry.

The proper human form for hundreds of thousands of years was always the 'clan'. A couple of dozen related individuals, a mobile extended family. (Interestingly, DNA studies show that most Paleolithic clans had one or two individuals of totally different genetic make-up, suggesting some restless souls ran off and found a better family!) Imagine how different life could be, if your days were spent immersed in the comfort, protection and help (and yes, crowdedness and lack of privacy) of at least a dozen people of every age, who loved you. And you were essential to their wellbeing too. How different parenthood would be, and childhood, and old age. How companionable.

Studies of time usage in contemporary hunter–gatherer societies reveal one more stunning thing. Feeding and clothing oneself took, at most, about three hours a day. When I read these studies, one thing just kept shouting at me – what losers we are! With our 50-hour work weeks, our mortgages and our collapsing ecosystems. There has to be a better way.

Forget Self-Help

We were designed to be in teams, of all ages and abilities, for life. Much of our Wild Creature Mind evolved for this social attunement. That is why it is our right brain that reads faces and body language, and sends messages back through our own face and stance, much more nuanced than words can do. (Go on Netflix and check out *Pride and Prejudice* – the Keira Knightley version. It's a miracle of non-verbal communication; faces say everything. A tilt of an eyebrow or the turn of a mouth signal subtlety and complexity that still makes sense. A five-year-old can tell if something is right or wrong. That's why they always know when we are lying.)

Left hemisphere could never organise something so complex! Imagine doing it from a list of instructions (raise eyebrows, scrunch forehead, emit sigh)!

Our pre-history was beautiful but also very dangerous and harsh. But emotional intelligence was our superpower, not claws or fangs. We can deal with anything, but *not on our own*. So please, dear reader, understand that while this is a book with a lot of information about how to help yourself, this is not a *self-help* book. This is a *help-each-other* book.

Relational approaches are now coming back into our language, especially around parenting. So our children feel 'seen'. That we 'hold a space' for them when they are upset or struggling to 'come to terms with' something like careless cruelty or fickle friends. Car stickers and campaigns urge us to listen and care about our mates at work, prompted by alarming incidence of male suicide, for example.

Social behaviours are all right hemisphere behaviours. Your Wild Creature Mind has the tools for this. So, dear reader, when you are talking to your loved ones or your workmates, or dealing with people out in the world, keep your felt sense going. Consult it quietly as you listen and speak. Pause often to allow its voice to come through to you, as Mary Hendricks Gendlin did to protect her baby from medical abuse. Your life is five times easier when you listen to your animal self. Elephants can show us the way!

AMAZING ELEPHANT FACTS

Elephants have been around (if you include their mastodon and mammoth forebears) for five million years. For an animal that is so different to us humans we have so much in common . . .

1. Elephants are good at health. They know lots of herbal remedies and self-administer them for various conditions. As far as we can find out, they don't write any of this down.

2. Less than five per cent of elephants get cancer. With humans, it's 25 per cent. Elephants have twenty varieties of the P53 gene, which prevents cancer. Humans only have two.

3. Female elephants, like female humans, stop reproducing at a certain point, and go into grandma mode. Only humans, elephants and orca whales do this. Grandma elephants hold enormous amounts of information about how to behave, where to go, how to solve problems of elephant life such as travel routes, and the care of the young. They actually retain internal maps of vast landscapes which the herd might traverse. (Presumably in their right

---

hemisphere.) Having a grandma elephant nearby for a young mother elephant will reduce the mortality of her young by *eightfold*. Yay for grandmas!

4. The behaviours that ensure survival are transmitted between elephants. They have a culture of how things are done, and they pass it on. An elephant with no family or tribe still has some basic urges, but they don't really work. An orphan elephant in Zimbabwe named Nzou lost all her family to poachers at the age of two. On reaching adulthood at 50, she adopted a tribe of buffalo and functioned as their leader. You make do with what you've got!

5. Elephants have wi-fi! Yes, they have an astonishing ability to network across large distances, by making loud (subsonic) sounds with their throats, which vibrate the ground all around, and create seismic signals that pass for miles underground. Elephant feet have extremely sensitive receptors on the edge of their 'soles' which can read these signals for detailed information about who is where, and what they are doing. The signals are processed as touch, but also go to the auditory nerve, bypassing the eardrum and straight into the elephant's Wild Creature Mind!

Elephant signalling includes passive signals – they eavesdrop on each other! And deliberate messaging, with warnings, mating calls and navigation instructions which can coordinate different groups across many miles. (Yes, okay, I can't resist it. It's Trunkbook!)

6. Finally, and I say this with fatalistic acceptance, elephants are matriarchal. Those big mothers call the shots. They just know best, and it's best to go along. Young males are often kicked out, wander in family-like groups with other young males for comfort, and one day win their way back into a herd if they are well-behaved. And as I wrote in *Raising Boys,* they need male role models to get it right, or they became chess sets and piano keys.

It all adds up to a species that is astonishingly socially aware, in touch and helping each other.

Who is Around

There is one more thing to know about 'being there' for each other. There was always a massive puzzle about PTSD – how come some people get it, and others don't? The latest trauma research has revolutionised our understanding of this and rewritten the playbook on how to care for post-traumatic injury sufferers. In short, it's not what happens to you; it's *who was around when it happened.*

With the right care available – real human, intimate care – the processing happens on the spot, before it can become a problem (as Peter Levine's story showed, on page 206).

We are not meant to do life alone. Our current culture of individualism, of life as a contest – or 'rugged' individualism, if you are male – might well explain our terrible outcomes with trauma in soldiers, emergency workers and medical staff. The culture around them is two-thirds of the problem. Wild Creature Mind signals – by letting your body know what feels right and wrong and by noticing the faces and voice tone of your colleagues – help you retribalise your consciousness, to become more of a 'we' and less of a 'me'. It is the key to good teamwork.

How Social Support Works

Julie Perrin is an Australian writer and storyteller with a beautiful touch. I get both nourishment and insight from her stories. If you have lost a parent, you will know it can be very hard to manage funerals and finances and everything else when you are floored by grief and just want to curl up somewhere and have it all go away. But Julie was surprised by where help comes from – and how much difference it makes.

TELLING AURELIA – BY JULIE PERRIN

In the week following my mother's funeral I wake up knowing I need to begin cooking again. For all of January my mother's death has been my whole world. In the small hiatus between the bushfires and the Coronavirus lockdown, we've had the privilege of a communal farewell.

But now the gifts of home-made food have slowed. I have wound a cocoon around keeping vigil and arranging the funeral; it is time to come out. I need to enter the world beyond my door. It takes me until lunchtime to coax myself from under the doona. I will walk up to the local shops for bread and vegetables.

The Italian fruit and veggie shop has an open storefront facing the street. I recognise Aurelia as she stands in the aisle, lightly stacking gleaming fruit. She has worked here for as long as I can remember, though she only appears to be in her early forties. She wears a navy blue uniform stitched with lime green highlights. It bears the names of the brothers who own the business.

As I approach her in the narrow aisle, Aurelia is deftly placing plums. Her coral pink fingernails flash amidst the dark purple. She turns towards me with a bird-like quickness in the movement of her head. Her hair is full of impish drama, the top sticks straight up, the sides are close cut. When Aurelia cocks her head to one side, her bright eyes meet my gaze. I realise I've felt on my guard coming out into the world again, but here is curiosity and kindness. Aurelia's eyes are alive and alert, undimmed by years of customer interactions.

The colour and sheen of the shop gleam under bright lights, the air is fresh. I have been feeling hidden, but Aurelia's presence welcomes me back. Her face is mobile, attentive, there is no risk her strong make-up will mask her loveliness. The clean lines of her eyebrows, cheekbones and lips are accented and clear. 'Hello,' she says, 'how are you?' Aurelia stands back and rocks on her heels as she says this, then grounds her two feet slightly apart. Her ready stance tells me she means the question.

I realise I want her to know that my mother has died. I don't need her to do anything, just know. I tell her Mum had a good death at the end of a long life. There is a pause that marks this new absence. Aurelia is perfectly tuned. Her eyes rest on me as she asks, 'Are you okay?'

Standing next to the fruit stack, Aurelia tells me about her grandfather's death in Italy. She had visited him there many times but could not be there when he was dying. She rang while the family was gathered. Someone held the phone to his ear. Her grandfather said her name. 'Aurelia.' And then he said, 'Goodbye Aurelia.' Later she learned these were the only words he spoke in the last weeks of his life.

'You take care now,' she says as she gently straightens my collar.

The evening Mum died, when it was finally time to leave the hospital, I stood in the corridor, outside her room. A nurse came to farewell me. She held a clipboard in one hand but with the other she reached up and patted down my crooked collar. Sometimes this would feel patronising, but not in these moments. I am one of the motherless now, the gesture is instinctively soothing.

When I am about to leave the shop, I look for Aurelia to give her a wave, but she's gone out the back. It doesn't matter. The transaction is complete. Something important in each of our lives is known to the other. Aurelia's shining listening and quiet telling have allowed me to re-enter the world. In returning to ordinary life I don't need to feel I am betraying or ignoring what has happened. One person in this shopping strip knows my truth.

I step out into the street, my collar neatly arranged, salad veggies and a ciabatta loaf swinging in my shoulder bag.

So there we go.

An elephant drapes a trunk. A life-filled woman holds space when it is badly needed and anchors it with a touch. How connected we are, and need to be.

The reality for elephants and humans is that we are barely individuals at all. That aloneness is unnatural and threatening – think of the mass shooters craving internet fame, or the sad and lonely incels typing at their screens. The sexual predators transforming their own needs for intimacy into violence inflicted on terrified victims. As I wrote in my book *Manhood* long ago, when people become unwoven from the fabric of human belonging, they pose an immense danger.

HOW WE GOT TO BE SO SOCIAL

Archaeology has uncovered a clear sequence in our evolution that tells us a great deal about who we are today. Spoken language in our ancestors arose only *after* we mastered fire. From this revolution, two things changed. With fire, we could cook and so digest far more food with less effort, making it possible for our brains to grow. And grow they did. We now sat around those fires for warmth and protection from predators, and that meant we were face-to-face. And it was only then that spoken language exploded – we know this from changes to the throat, and concomitant changes to the architecture of our ears, maximising hearing of voice sounds. Our primate relatives lived in groups too, but not like this. They were all dominated by single, larger males. In this era, we moved towards greater equality. We paired up. We were collaborators. We suddenly could plan and work as one in a way that even the best lion pride or wolf pack could not match.

'Less me, more we' is the key to happiness

There are cultures and languages in various parts of the world that have no word for 'me' or 'I'. That is an astounding difference in how the speaker thinks of themselves. These cultures, as you might guess, are all pre-industrial, forager cultures; the shape of being human for 95 per cent of our history. *The norm for being human is being part of a group.*

The emotion we call shame also arose out of this intense dependence on the group. Shame is what we feel when we know, sometimes suddenly, that we have endangered a bond – let down our partner or children or friends. It sweeps the body, is unmistakable to see, and it sends a signal of remorse, which in turn is the first step to repair. In my book *Raising Girls*, a father who has not 'been there' for his daughter encounters an explosion of hurt one day, where she lists the times he has let her down, going back to early primary school. His first impulse is to justify himself – in effect, to strike back – but he has the backbone to not do that, to stand in the fire of her pain and hurt, and to be profoundly sorry. Shame shows in our face and our posture, and that is what the

246

other person needs to see; *that their pain matters*. This is the beginning of the fabric being woven back into place.

Shame evolved in times when a person might be driven out of the clan if they behaved selfishly or without care for the safety of others. In the Neolithic, being driven from the clan could easily be a death sentence. For males especially, the emotion of shame became hardwired to be so aversive that it sometimes outranked death or injury. 'Death before dishonour.' Belonging is a primary need.

LETTING THE LOVE IN

I was flipping pages in *The Body Keeps the Score* – a wonderful but dense book about trauma by Bessel van der Kolk. This paragraph leaped out:

> Social support is not the same as merely being in the presence of others. The critical issue is reciprocity: being truly heard and seen by the people around us, feeling that we are held in someone's mind and heart. For our physiology to calm down, heal and grow we need a visceral feeling of safety. No doctor can write a prescription for friendship and love. These are complex and hard-earned capacities.

We need to unpack what he means by 'reciprocity'. It isn't a quid pro quo, like paying the counsellor for seeing you! Reciprocity in relationships begins with a mother and baby. The baby depends utterly on its mother for all its needs – touch, nourishment, comfort. The mother provides these as best she can. The baby feels better. Mother and baby gaze at each others' faces. Perhaps the baby makes some happy sounds. By responding to the care, the baby is 'reciprocating'. It encourages the mother, often fragile in her new role, and she grows more confident.

A counsellor friend of mine had a client who was very stuck and caught in self-pity. Gradually, they were making a connection, but still, they wondered – am I really helping?

One day, their client said, 'Thank you for hanging in with me.' It felt like a breakthrough. They were acknowledging that they felt the relatedness. That it was impactful. And so they were 'letting the love in' – which is the role of a baby with a mother. This is reciprocity. And they felt for the first time they were on the right track.

What we need from each other is not complicated, it's really just to keep trying.

My teachers Bob and Mary Goulding would give praise to us as trainees and be alert to how we received it. If we tried to brush it off, they would look sternly at us and restate the praise. Our job was to allow it to have impact, to let our bodies soften and stand tall with it. If you are dealing with a loved one who is stuck in self-pity or low self-esteem, it's helpful to challenge them: 'I am loving you, and caring for you. Your job is to notice that.'

There are animals which are not social at all. Wombat babies are closely bonded to their mums, but all wombat mums are single mums! And a grown wombat loves to live alone, building little Lego stacks with its rectangular poo to warn off intruders. But humans are social, and along with elephants, orcas, lions and many others, we basically only thrive when we are in a group. Solitary humans do exist, but they are mostly having a massive, lifelong sulk. Which when you think about it, is a very social thing to do!

Wild Creature Mind is highly developed for making sociability easier and more successful. We take eighteen years or so to raise our young, we form long-term pair bonds with varying degrees of success and we need friends and a wider community to really have good mental health. This takes a lot of skill, maturity, and especially one key understanding . . . that *we are not in this world for ourselves.* (We have and hold our boundaries, not with the aim of separation, but of better engagement – being unentangled makes the best intimacy.)

We have the most fun, make our best contribution and live the longest, healthiest lives when we value and love others as much as ourselves.

Summing Up

Our culture began to fragment into lonely and dysfunctional lives around the same time we lost our awareness of our right hemisphere, our antenna to the matrix that is the living world. Falling in love again with our fellow humans, and with nature, is easy when our right brain is guiding us. Our Wild Creature Mind will always bring us back home.

Today we hold our independence very dearly, and would be terrified to be so interdependent – and constrained – as in a hunter–gatherer world. We would not choose to go totally back to such a culture. But perhaps just halfway?

What would it feel like, to be so unanxious, so unalone, so cherished? What would it be like if every teenager felt needed and valuable? Every child loved by a dozen adults? Every old person revered and cared for until they choose freely the time of their leaving?

Probably, it would feel a bit like being an elephant.

Chapter 15

A Lion at Sunset

The sun is setting over the rocky bluffs and peaks which edge Africa's Great Rift Valley. The grassy plains below are unique in the history of the earth – the cradle of an immense procession of species, including, of course, our own.

The great star's red glow reflects in the rheumy eyes of an ageing lion sprawled atop a boulder, gazing out across the plains. In its peripheral vision, it can see its own extended family, well fed, resting and content. The hunt has gone well, rains have brought green grass, new cubs are nuzzling at their mothers' teats.

The old lion does not think to itself, as we might, 'Nice sunset', but on a deeper level, it registers a complex number of factors which add up to 'job done'.

It is lucky to have no sense of time or history. This scene could be any point in the five million years that lions have been around. Our own history only stretches back one tenth of that. The world of a lion is essentially timeless. They know how to chill.

We've been on such an epic journey together, dear reader, and much wild country has been crossed. And you've made it, so *congratulations*! Take a second to feel proud (and to notice where that feeling lives in your body, ha ha!)

It all might seem like a jumble of memories right now, so many stories and ideas. So in this final chapter I want to tie it all together, by flying over that country, helicopter-style, for one last look. Here goes.

We started the book with a young girl in a bad place. Ellie was not far from needing hospital admission, medication, perhaps even suicide-watch and a long road back. Instead, she found someone able to steady her and help her get back into her body. We only saw Ellie take the very first step – *she fully took on the idea of having a Wild Creature inside.*

Ellie experienced this in two specific ways:

1. There was a tender small creature part of her, which was in need of her care. Just knowing this triggered something innate. Instead of being trapped in the frightened victim place, Ellie was springboarded into being a protector. This is one consequence of that wonderful way of conceptualising distress – that 'there is something in me'. No longer swamped by her emotions, Ellie could experience herself as a capable person, looking after something vulnerable and precious. Ellie

254

was tending herself, which she was perfectly equipped to do.

2. Paradoxically, there was also inside her a ferocious, savvy and powerful animal ally. She could feel it stirring. (You have felt this, dear reader, I am sure. Mothers or fathers reading this may have, before parenthood, been the mildest and most inoffensive, compliant souls, but with a small baby to protect, we find we have access to homicidal levels of protective rage.) Ellie would tap into this more and more, with the therapist's help, locating it in her body from small cues until it emerged fully grown. Fangs bared.

Wild Creature methods are not about sedating us to the horrors of the world; in fact, they do the complete opposite. So it's time to catch you up with what happened next.

In her third interview with the therapist, Ellie disclosed something that she had never been willing to tell her parents. (Like many girls of her age, she did not want to be even more of a worry to them. And also like many of her generation, she had come to believe this was simply the way the world was, and that she had to 'suck it up'.)

Ellie told her therapist that most afternoons after school, she and her friends were being sexually harassed by some older private school boys at the bus interchange. The boys would circle around them, make sexualised comments or requests of them, always framed as joking, though their body language was anything but friendly. Sometimes the boys would have ugly and graphic pornographic images on their phones and push them in the girls' faces. Ellie had found she was trembling uncontrollably after some of these exchanges and was having nightmares about them. One or two of Ellie's friends at first thought it was exciting to have the attention of these well-off older boys. But soon they all found it intimidating, exhausting and demoralising.

Talking to her counsellor and listening to her own body, Ellie found herself growing enraged, instead of frightened, and determined to do something about this.

She told her friends that she was going to tell her parents, and they should do the same. Within days, the girls and their parents would meet with their school principal to seek her help. Within 24 hours, the principal met with the principal of the boys' school. It might have resulted in a token response – some platitudes about respect at a school assembly. But in this case, a real fire was lit. The adults had found their backbone. Because the events had happened in a public place, it was potentially a police matter. The boys' parents were contacted and presented with the problem. They would be required to arrange a different way for their sons to get home from school, the boys would not be using that bus stop again. The girls did not set aside their rights to take further action involving the police. But they had made a start. Back in Ellie's school, the story spread like wildfire. Hundreds of girls walked a little taller. Boys within the co-ed school too had to reflect on their own behaviour. Ellie, in the weeks that followed, became a different girl who met your gaze and held her head high.

Young people's mental health problems are often located not in the child, but in the world we have built around them. If we addressed pornography use, if we acted on the climate apocalypse looming in these kids' futures, if we kept social media out of their lives until their late teens, then they would be able to have the childhoods that they need to grow happy and strong. I hope that you can feel in your body the heat and power of wanting this to be so.

There is something else important to add here. The uses of the right hemisphere are not simply to reach some kind of stasis or resolution, because that isn't how life works. Eugene Gendlin, wearing his philosopher's hat, said often that the mind, and in fact our own whole organism, is a 'movement forward', that life itself is implicitly about 'unfolding'. It doesn't stop. (That is why it is so exciting to be alive, and so mighty a journey to see where it all might go.)

Imagine then, that Ellie in her fourth session with the therapist, after the bus-stop business has been resolved, is asked this question: 'Ellie, how are you now? What is happening in your body when you sit with the "everything" of what has happened?'

And – after a pause – Ellie's answer is: 'There is an ache, a kind of tightness around my heart.' And as they know the routine well now, the two of them sit with that, to see what comes to mind. And then it comes: Ellie sees a face. It is the face of one of the boys.

'There was one of the boys, one of that group, who was never mean to us. He always looked uncomfortable about how the others were acting. I can see his face, once he looked right at me, and I can see that look now. He is looking right at me, like he is so ashamed. That's what goes with the hurting around my heart.'

And lets imagine what the therapist asks next. 'What are you thinking now, Ellie, as you see him again?'

Ellie goes quiet, the therapist waits quietly with her.

Then the answer comes: 'I am worried about him.'

'Can you say what the worry is?'

'I . . . I'm worried that he might kill himself. Does that sound crazy?'

'No,' the therapist replies.

Imagine that the two of them agree upon some action. That the therapist, who has a very strong ethic about how she goes about her work, contacts the counselling team at the school the boy attends. (It's a fancy school, it has a team!) The boy is quietly invited to meet with a counsellor, and he is astonishingly frank, perhaps because he has been told why the enquiry is taking place. Yes, he has considered taking his life. And things begin to swing into action. An offer is relayed for Ellie to meet with the boy, with their two therapists present, and in that meeting they find that they have much to share. He is profoundly upset by having been one of the group, even though he did not join in the harassment, and Ellie reassures him.

Imagine they become good friends, and in the years that follow their friendship grows, with an idealistic core to their relationship that is a bulwark against the ugliness of much that goes on in the world around them. In the late 2020s, they will be part of a six-million young-person blockade around the world of 'carbon criminal' corporations. It will last for six weeks, shutting down whole city blocks and many large airports, and proves a turning point in many governments being able to take proper measures – belatedly – to mitigate the unfolding disasters, which are so in evidence, at the cause. What is astonishing about these changes is the almost complete lack of violence and the support of millions of their grandparents generation. It is a unique collaboration of old and young; a defining moment in history. Imagine.

The Voice Inside You

Our next leg of the journey was a deep dive into brain structure. Remember that diagram on page 21? As you gazed at all those nerves spreading down into our bodies, I wanted you to actually feel them in yourself, because they were your own aliveness.

This is more radical an act than you might think. Our culture treats you like a machine. It's even the way we were taught science in the past – body as merely a vehicle for your brain, universe as random emptiness (a fact that makes Iain McGilchrist furious, as it so contradicts the way both our mind and the cosmos works). Caught in this 19th century idea of how things work – it's not surprising that we treat ourselves the same way. And each other.

Instead, I wanted you to be in awe of the miracle that was your own inner process. Stirring, surging, interacting with the life force around you. I wanted you to feel larger than you had thought you were. And to notice that, down in your torso and throughout your body, you vibrate with connection to the living world of animals, plants, stars and sky. And even in the most prosaic things, your body is a signalling device from your right hemisphere, your animal knowledge and memory giving you insights and a path forward in your own unfolding.

Your right hemisphere, ultimately, is a spiritual organ. Walk with Indigenous people on Country, they are trance-like yet totally aware. They are in Wild Creature Mind continually. Merging, not dominating, not merely observing, they *are* the land. What Barry Lopez in *Arctic Dreams* describes as 'wearing the landscape like clothing'.

Stephen and Ondrea Levine were Buddhist teachers who set up a phone service for people facing death or grief, in the 1970s. One of their callers was Dorothy, a mother whose nine-year-old daughter was dying of lymphoma. Even though her child now had large swellings on her body, and the lymphoma was clearly very advanced, Dorothy was unable to tell her daughter she was dying. Stephen, after a long discussion with her, asked Dorothy to focus on the centre of her chest, and to breathe into it, almost like there was a vent into her heart. That 'all sorts of images might arise, glimpses of the deaths of others, and the hard swallowing of long-held tears'. To be willing to be in this pain because beneath it was the vast love she felt for her daughter. And by facing and feeling this pain, she could lower the walls between her daughter and her, so that in the limited time they had left, their love would be unshielded and complete. It is so very important that we don't let pain stop us from loving. And this becomes something tangible and physical which we can do, using the body's signals and sending our acceptance and openness to help them shift.

We use our left brain to reach out to our right. When we use words to guess at the meaning of a sensation, then that sensation can clarify. Both sides of your brain 'get' each other, and combine their unique strengths.

Even thinking of a person you care about evokes a felt sense of where you are, relationally, with that person. Felt sense is always fresh, it has something new to tell you and, if you keep that channel open, it becomes a way to guide you. So you can relate to the real them, with the real you, each time you meet.

This is the day-to-day usefulness of this skill. Having Wild Creature activated as you talk to your children, or reconnect with your partner at the end of the day, makes it much more likely to go well. (How often, I hear you thinking, does it not work, as we jar and jolt with each other and feel rushed and unsatisfied, and before you know it, the world's rush has swept you apart again.) Intimacy is essential nourishment for human beings. It makes our kids grow up strong and calm, makes our partnerships alive and restorative, our love lives exciting and soul nurturing. And you can only be intimate when your Wild Creature is right there in the room. Intimacy isn't the rubbing together of facts!

We were introduced to the pioneers of the neuroscience, to reassure your left hemisphere that this all stacked up. It often made me smile in the years I was working this all out. That Iain McGilchrist, whose left-brain command of neuroscience was almost without peer, discovered the astonishing silence of the right brain in our modern minds. He made an impassioned plea to revive it if we were to survive, though he was not specific as to how this could be done.

Eugene and Mary Gendlin, Ann Weiser Cornell and the worldwide focusing community had been working on how to listen to our 'felt sense' for nearly sixty years. They had very little science behind why this worked. (Though Leslie Ellis was pioneering that; her papers are quite wonderful.)

Focusing practitioners were having a modest influence on the therapy scene, and some warm and grounded people were doing wonderful work. But most people had not heard of them.

McGilchrist's world and Gendlin's world needed to meet up. That seemed a job that had fallen to me. I and a few others were clear that *felt sense was the voice of right brain* and that this Wild Creature capacity, to live intelligently without words, could turbo-charge the experience of being human from its desiccated state in modern corporatised life.

We needed to break out of the old mythical paradigm – left brain as intelligent and rational, right brain as emotional and artistic – and see that left brain was a bossy pedant which, when left to its own devices, was defensive, distorted the facts and was prone to tantrums. We needed to comprehend that the right brain was more grounded in reality, complex enough to manage an ambiguous, subtle and nuanced world of relationships, ecologies and collaborative community.

And then we met James. In his first appearance in the book, he taught us about the simplest and most everyday uses of Wild Creature Mind. When unhappy, restless, tense, unable to sleep or in any way out of sorts, there is a protocol that will always help.

Notice you are feeling bad.

Say 'there is something in me'.

Locate where it lives, sense its shape and quality.

Tell it both 'welcome' and 'thank you'.

Soften around it to give it room.

Try out a word or two to describe it. This word or two will never be quite right on first go.

Try a better word, and listen to see if your felt sense says, 'Yes.'

And then, in the way that we sometimes have to just abandon control in order for anything magical to happen – to dance, to make love with abandon, to laugh, to play great music – *you just let what comes come.*

James was only helped to get to sleep that night, not cured. That would need the help of someone who could hold space for him with infinite care. After several days, his therapist and he entered into the heart of the matter, guided by his body. They found that his Wild Creature Mind had done some important work below the level of awareness. It had stored and sequenced his traumatic career, and found the pivotal harm he had sustained. A terrible tragedy, especially for a loving father. A little girl whose body had been injured beyond saving. This girl had touched his soul; they had bonded even as her life was fading out.

Once James and Ange knew what the matter was, it wasn't hard to find a way forward. James needed to weep the anguish out right there in the room, and knew down inside that he needed to make a restorative ritual at little

Karina's graveside. He had to open his heart in hell and find that it was still loving and strong. He would have so much more to give the world.

Writing this book, I felt a deep sense of relief when James's story was written down. I knew you would understand it, and it would carry all these abstract concepts into real life. And that you had a tool now, whether you were a teenager or a struggling adult hammered by life circumstances or you did an intense and dangerous job. You had a pathway to heal life's terrors, and not be taken down by them.

Now we had the big boulders in place, we could attend to lots of the applications of Wild Creature/felt sensing to everyday life.

Boundaries were a big one. Mary, as a young new mother, fighting off the arsehole pediatrician who was stealing blood for his research, causing needless pain to newborn babies. Mary made it clear that we don't have to be brave or loud by nature – we can get strength simply by giving ourselves permission to pause. In that pause, Wild Creature can come out of the thickets, shake itself off and snarl.

We moved onto children. Kids are so open to their Wild Creature, they delightfully access it, since they haven't yet had to stuff it into a cage. Sophie's mum helped her find what was behind her pain – not a grazed knee, but a wounded sense of worth. Ravi's mum, likewise, so cleverly

265

used those simple directions which you too can have in your armoury:

Can you feel inside where that bad feeling is?

Can you describe it, how it feels, what shape it is? What it is doing?

And then, pivotally: *What do you think it is wanting to say to you?*

If all else fails, get out the pens and paints and draw it, taking as long as you need. Talk to your child from time to time about how it is going.

It is important to really settle in while doing this, it can't be rushed. Be patient, breathing slow, helping your child to stay with it. Again, the little Wild Creature comes out of the bushes.

Whenever we learn a skill, we need a plan for if it doesn't work. This was where Sally came in – the writer to the *Guardian* advice page. The 'good daughter' who couldn't shake her anger, because she actually had not listened to it at all. Her Wild Creature stayed angry for 30 years until she finally faced up to her dad being a selfish so-and-so (which we have all been sometimes) who had driven a truck through her childhood.

There are many ways that our bodies can help us, and many modalities which can help elicit this. Contacting Wild Creature can trigger in us some very physical reactions. We burst into tears, flush with rage, wash with sorrow, shake as we release held-in fear.

From the nightmare of war and dislocation called the 20th century (and now, so sadly, reaching into the 21st), many of our muscles and nerves are permanently locked in fright. Talking on its own will barely touch these. So TRE trembling comes into its own as a simple physical practice. Lie down, angle your legs and start to wobble and shake. Let it into your whole self. (Like everyone's favourite part of the 'Hokey Pokey', you put your whole self in!) I processed the after effects of a crappy surgical procedure in childhood, but only 60 years later. We can do this sooner in ourselves and our kids. It's so simple.

The dream chapter was a late addition – I only came across the luminous Leslie Ellis at the last minute, and she was a revelation. Nightmares are a very upsetting thing, and we have long searched for a remedy. Focusing approaches are far superior to most other methods. By identifying the helper figure hidden in every dream, or if we are braver, the 'opposite to us' figure, we can then apply Wild Creature awareness to flesh them out and own them more. We can eat our shadow and become larger selves.

Our right hemisphere knows how to manage disparate and contradictory things, it is superbly non-binary. When we use felt sense around fragmented parts of our psyche, it effortlessly begins to meld them in. There is no part of you that is bad, or not helpful, once it is properly digested into the wholeness of you.

Finally, we had some fun with elephants, my favourite

animal because they are actually SO human. They live *the way we should live* – in extended families who share the parenting, amble through the world and have wi-fi that goes through their feet! They share their lives on Trunkbook!

So, dear reader, we got there. I hope you can see it all fitting together, and being quite simple and elegant. Not at all hard to put into action, especially as you've been doing that all the way through.

To check, just ask yourself:

Do you notice your felt sense more often?

Do you use the focusing sequence when you are unhappy or stuck?

Are you shifting to being more in your right hemisphere as a way of life: open and aware of your body as life happens? (i.e. Are you happy to love and be loved, and less driven to acquire status or possessions? Do you engage in purposes that are bigger than yourself, with a peaceful heart and happy resolve?)

If that is even starting in a tiny way for you, dear reader, then I am happy beyond words. And if not, well, it's not too late. Keep at it.

You are a graduate of this book!

A hundred years from now, a Wild Creature emerges from some leafy cover.

They glance back and make a sound, and some small young creatures tumble into the light. If we are lucky, if we get it right, they are human beings. If we are *really* lucky, there will still be hospitals and music, aircraft and elephants. We'll have made it through.

A Personal Last Word

It's clear, looking back on a long life, that there were some simple stages.

As a small child, though there were sometimes fears, the world felt rather marvellous and I was part of everything.

Then came school and the big world, and a kind of anxiety that never went away. Would I be good enough, would I belong, would I fail at everything and humiliation be my life?

Then, gradually, things improved.

But now, in old age, some of those fears return, and so I seek refuge. We all need refuge, if we are to rest and return to be part of the caring for others that we are in this world to give.

So here is a prayer to recite:

I take refuge in two things which are certain.
I feel them in my body, I know them in my mind.
All life is sacred.
All life is one.
And that includes me.

There is much to be grateful for, even in a time of loss.
I breathe, in and out. I feel my body, its gentle aliveness.
I surrender into the loving arms of the great mother.
One small Wild Creature coming home.

Exercises for Listening to Wild Creature Mind

These exercises are designed to help you to notice and track your Wild Creature felt sense more easily, and become familiar with how it changes and moves in your body. As you start to do this, the miracle of neuroplasticity – new linkages growing stronger with practice – will make it easier and easier.

The best way to do the exercises is to read each one first, and as they are really very simple, just do that one from memory. Once you have got one mastered, then try another.

Of course, as you read them, they will very likely start happening. Just give yourself time to experience the exercise, for as long as you like. I am grateful to Dr Leslie Ellis in Canada for some of the exercises. Leslie says that doing them is rather like those old polaroid photos – the instant photos, which start out murky and become clearer in a few seconds time. That's the nature of felt sense, it grows as you attend to it. Your Wild Creature comes out of the bushes!

1. SOMETHING YOU LOVE

For this exercise, choose either a person whom you love, or have warm or appreciative feelings towards.

Just picture that person, think of them and then – notice down the front and middle of your body, as well as anywhere else, the sensations that happen in your body.

Where do you notice those sensations?

How would you describe them?

If you have time, repeat this for a PLACE you love. How is that different? And an OBJECT or possession which matters to you?

How is that different?

2. A BIT OF TROUBLE

For this exercise, choose a small area of your life which at the moment is problematic – nothing too severe. Think about that problem, annoyance or difficulty.

Notice what happens in your body when you do that?

Where do sensations happen?

How would you describe them?

Now, when that is clear and reasonably defined, imagine sending that problem further away from you – a few miles away (you might have to be imaginative with this). Just make the problem more distant in any way you can.

Notice what happens in your body when you do that.

How the original sensations change, if they do.

3. LETTING WILD CREATURE DECIDE

Settle down in a chair, and clear some space in your mind. Look at a few objects around you, listen for any sounds in your environment. Shuffle a bit to get comfortable if you need to, then bring your attention back to yourself.

Ask yourself this question – 'What in my life needs my attention right now?'

Notice what comes up. It might be obvious, or it might be a bit surprising. Just trust what your mind is popping up in answer to this question.

Notice what happens in your body as you think of this aspect, question or development.

Where are the sensations located?

Can you make them 'welcome', i.e. have a friendly and open feeling towards them, that they want to help you?

How would you describe them, in vague terms?

As you try out those words, do better words come to mind, slightly more accurate, to describe the actual sensation?

Keep updating your descriptions, as the sensations change or solidify or move and shift.

Be open to where they travel, or want to go and allow that as best you can.

Notice anything else that comes into your mind, as you do this.

Eventually bring yourself back to the outer world, the comfiness of the chair, any sounds you can hear, objects you can see.

4. BOUNDARIES

To develop good boundaries, the first step is always to have a pause. Whenever 'put on the spot', give yourself permission, and specifically ask for a moment to think about it. Here are some nice clear instances to practise.

First we will go for a YES example.

a. Your much-loved friend has just had you to a delicious lunch, and you've spent an afternoon talking about old times. They ask if you can take a photo of them and their new cat to send to their grandchildren.

- What sensations happen in your body.
- Where are they located?
- (This is a baseline situation – so you know what YES feels like too.)

b. Imagine you are at a playground. There are a few children playing, and a few mums and dads there as well. A person comes up to you and asks you to mind their three children. They just need to quickly drive home and get their cigarettes.
   - What sensations happen in your body?
   - Where are they located?

c. A politician you can't stand the sight of comes to your town after massive fires destroyed much of your community, including the homes of some of your dearest friends. (If you are in the UK, insert floods for fires!) He went overseas secretly in the middle of fire season and ignored the warnings of fire chiefs for a year leading up to the fires, refusing even to meet with them. He has done nothing ever about climate change, and in fact mocks those who do. But now he is here seeking a photo op. He has a posse of photographers with him. He wants to shake your hand.
   - What sensations happen in your body?
   - Where are they?

d. Someone you are on good terms with urges you to have another glass of wine. You have to drive soon, and have already had two drinks.

- What sensations happen in your body?
- Where are they located?

Do you have a clearer sense of what yes, and no, feel like in your body? Were there differences between the examples?

5. A 'FISHING EXPEDITION' EXERCISE

Use this to smoke out what your Wild Creature thinks of situations, by making a very bald and extreme statement.

For example:

Everything in my life is wonderful, and I know the future will be just great.

- What sensations happen in your body?
- Where are they?

You can also do this for specific situations.

For example:

- I am completely at ease about our holiday arrangements.

- I have complete confidence in the builders who will build our new house with all our life savings.
- My marriage/relationship is perfect in every way.
- I am completely blameless in how things in my life have gone pear-shaped.

Wild Creature can be heard snorting in each instance. Notice where it is located, and the quality of the sensations. How do they change or progress as you notice? What thoughts do they lead to, as your left and right brains start to discuss it?

6. ALL THE WAY TO HEAVEN

Imagine that the day-to-day problems of your life manage to be gradually resolved. They turn out to have been okay after all – things worked out! Notice what happens in your body when you imagine that. Take a few seconds to let that feeling grow. Now, imagine that in the big world, all the concerns that impinge on us – politics, climate, crime, war, poverty, disease – have gradually been overcome, and we reach a golden time for the human race and the natural world of harmony and exuberant aliveness. Imagine! Can you sense in your body how it would be if it were so? Let that feeling grow inside you and see what it is like. The peace that lies underneath our struggles is always there, and we need to know that.

I hope you've had fun with these exercises, and they have lit up some new neurons which will stay switched on to help you be more fully alive. And huge gratitude to Ann Weiser Cornell and Leslie Ellis and others who devised them.

Final Thoughts

It was very important to me, in writing *Wild Creature Mind*, that I made it a simple and easy read. So that anyone, from any age or level of education, could enjoy the book. I hope I came close – and in your case, dear reader, perhaps I did, because, well – here you are!

Of course, that approach has a downside. Going for an effortless read meant leaving out anything too wide-ranging or too tangled or wild. So lots of fun stuff was kept back. This special section – for the very keen reader – allows me to add some of that. If you dip in and like it, well, it's a free bonus and will help you to 'bed in' the messages of the book. Also, sometimes, when you have finished a good movie or novel, you just don't want it to end! If you aren't ready to quit yet, neither am I.

A Poem To Begin

There is a long tradition of having a quote – called an epigraph – at the start of a book. Ideally, it encapsulates or at least hints at what the whole book is about; saying, in effect, I am not the first to think this way. Here is some notable person who agrees.

To save you riffling back, here it is again.

You only have to let the soft animal of your body
Love what it loves.

I am in awe of this quote, and the poem that it comes from, because it gently opens a door to a different way of being in the world. It does in fifteen words what the entire book attempts, but possibly better!

Mary Oliver died in 2019 at the age of 84, probably the best loved American poet of her time. I think her secret was that she put people in touch with their Wild Creature selves. She herself certainly was – fiercely alive, deeply engaged with the natural world and strong and clear in her approach to life, both its joy and its pain.

Google her and you can see her lined and friendly face, no-nonsense haircut and an unflinching but soft-eyed gaze. Mary read this poem 'Wild Geese' in a rare interview, for the radio program *On Being*, which you can listen to on YouTube. Here are the closing words:

Whoever you are, no matter how lonely,
the world offers itself to your imagination,
calls to you like the wild geese, harsh and exciting,

over and over announcing your place in the family
of things.

Isn't that just awesome?

I can remember hearing wild birds calling in the
night as a teenager in the Carrum marshes south-east of
Melbourne. I'd been abandoned by my parents and raised
myself on crawdads. (No, I made that part up. But it was
a sound that made you know you had instincts.) Neil
Young's haunting song 'Helpless' (easily found on Spotify
or YouTube, in concert with The Band, and Joni Mitchell
doing exquisite harmony) expresses the yearning to be
back there again, in the freshness of being young.

Our senses, if we attend to them, pull us directly into
our right hemisphere. Our Wild Creature Mind stretches
its limbs and wakes up. Even if the world we live in is man-
made, it still works, we are like a fox in a city street at
night; every nerve-ending fully alive. Occupy your senses
every chance you get, it will always steady you, either
through calmness, if there is no real danger, or resolve, if
you need to gird up and fight.

Mary's poem ends by promising something deeper –
to include you in the family of things. And 'No matter
how lonely' – what a claim that is! This is personal,
dear reader – curious teenager, harassed parent, wary
oldster. This is no small thing. Loneliness is the root
cause of almost all the evil out there in the world, the

underpinnings of greed, violence, sexual predation, every kind of destructiveness.

Like that shrivelled man who murdered British MP Jo Cox, a mum of two small children and an icon of overseas aid work so significant that President Obama telephoned her husband personally to share his grief. The police described the killer as 'never having held a job, never had a girlfriend, never any friends to speak of'. Our crime, our complicity in this, is that we let little boys grow up this way. Knowing only coldness, their hearts turning to stone, their yearnings for closeness twisting into blind and pointless rage.

Being trapped in left hemisphere, with no heart connection, underlies all terrors. People whose Wild Creatures have been silenced can only walk the earth like zombies. But Wild Creature Mind brings us back into caring for each other. Our nature as humans is to connect and nurture. Personal despair is dissolved when we remember that we are in this world for each other. It's not just that 'there are others worse off', as my mum used to say, but that they are living all around us, and self-absorption is a crime in a world of so much need that we can work to fill. Feeling sorry for yourself? Go and volunteer somewhere. All generosity flows both ways; your being kind nurtures you as well.

Rejoining the Wild and Loving World

Do *you* have 'a place in the family of things'? Well, of course you do. Loneliness is a yearning, and its existence implicitly arises from knowing that somewhere the object of its yearning must exist. To be held in the arms of the world.

When I sit with Shaaron, whom I have been with for over 50 years, we may talk, but that's only part of what it's about. Our relationship can be testing, and we can lose the plot, even after all this time. But something settles on us as we sit there, peace coming down like nightfall in the mountains. You breathe it.

If you want to get past a difference or difficulty with your partner, or just somehow realign with them at the end of a busy day, then talk, but not too much. Have some food, perhaps a drink. Then sit together quietly and wait for the peace to arrive. The trick is not to try to align with *them*, but to *align with yourself, as you sit with them*. Go to your felt sense. Your two Wild Creature Minds are already lining up, you just have to let them settle. It's the same with going into nature. Feel on the inside what is happening, as you walk those beaches or stride up those mountains. Doing this can multiply the benefits fivefold.

'The soft animal of your body'. How could it ever be expressed better than that? And how carefully chosen the words. Not 'do what it wants', but 'love what it loves'.

How trusting that inside us we seek only wholeness, and have no need to harm. Because we don't, we really don't.

So Why Poetry?

Few things illustrate our divided brain as much as the fact that we have two entirely different ways of using language. Poetry and prose.

Poetry is aimed at your right hemisphere, your 'wide open' mind, where newness – fresh experience – registers, and recognition takes place almost without thought. (Some say you only ever read a poem truly the first time, and it's the same with a piece of music, or a work of art. It absolutely penetrates your being with sudden understanding beyond words. All future enjoyment – considerable though it might be – is a memory of that first time.)

Poems are in right-brain language; they use rhythm and sound as much as vocabulary. They're full of metaphors and images, which the left hemisphere simply does not understand. (People with major damage to their right hemisphere lose all sense of story, imagery, irony or humour. They become like *Star Trek*'s Mr Spock, not comprehending anything that is implicit or subtle. Interestingly, Iain McGilchrist argues that many neurodivergent conditions involve problems in accessing the right hemisphere.)

Prose – the name we give to straightforward and linear language – is left hemisphere.

McGilchrist points out that language is not necessarily rational, it can be deceptive – as with slogans which make something complex sound simple. (My most hated slogan is 'stop the boats' because its appeal to simplicity put truly terrible people in charge of my country for almost ten years. What 'stop the boats' really means is 'die somewhere else'.) A logical-sounding idea can take whole countries towards madness: Build The Wall. Get Brexit Done. Lebensraum. This is why we so desperately need to use both hemispheres, because the world is not simple, and a well-lived life is almost always about finding creative ways through complex scenarios without reducing them to seemingly black-and-white choices. To generate new solutions means using both hemispheres.

Prose says, 'Winds varying from 25–40 kilometres per hour'. Poetry says, 'The moon was a ghostly galleon tossed upon cloudy seas'. One reminds you to close the door on your greenhouse. The other makes you want to leap onto a horse and go see the landlord's black-eyed daughter! It calls you to life. Listen to your left hemisphere. Go and close the greenhouse – you need to protect those tomato plants. But what are tomatoes if you are too distracted to taste their sweet, acid juiciness?

With brain hemispheres, you have to decide who to put in charge. Who is the master and who is the emissary?

The right hemisphere, speaking via your felt sense, has the big picture and was designed to keep you in harmony with the rest of the living world. *Meaning* (right brain) should precede *method* (left brain). What point in hard work, or effort, with no thought as to why? (This underlies much PTSD in soldiers – the compounding diagnosis of 'moral injury' – we fought well, but *for what*?) It's in our male nature to rush into a task without the proper thought. At least, it has been for the centuries since we abandoned our right brains.

Left hemisphere says *how* we can achieve a task; right asks 'why?' And in your life, overall, why is what matters most. No point in being wonderful at something that is pointless.

Two Minds in One Body

The idea of our having two minds living in one body is a pretty radical one. In fact, it can sound rather disconcerting! And yet it explains almost everything about being human, the more you think about it. It simply fits the evidence – explaining why for millions of people, out of touch with their own insides, mental wellbeing has been so elusive. And how quickly it returns once we befriend our animal side and build a relationship with it.

Psychiatrists in the past did have a name for the loss of Wild Creature functioning; even though they could not yet adequately explain it. They called it 'dissociation'. They did not have a word for dissociation's opposite though. It took the insights of teachers like Gautama Buddha to describe the true nature of being human. It is 'embodiment' – the proper activation of our right hemisphere through the practice of being deeply aware of one's own body and its intrinsic wisdom.

We all live on a continuum between dissociation and embodiment. We can at times be shockingly unaware of our senses, locked in left hemisphere isolation. It is of course a trauma response. It's possible to be home with one's family, cook food, earn a living, carry out many tasks, have sex and so on, while simply never being fully mentally present. It's an horrific experience for those around you who seek your presence, because they feel alone and unloved, and they are right. We need to work on embodiment, every second of every day, for our lives to go well. The only exception is doing your tax!

There are different aspects of being embodied, and different words to describe them.

There is *perception* – the input through our five senses of the world around us. This works for you when you enjoy art, or music or being at the beach, getting a massage, looking at flowers or playing with your pet cat or dog.

There is *proprioception* – knowing how we are positioned – where our hands are or our legs or feet (and perhaps moving them about to express ourselves). So yoga, dance, exercise, running and walking, Tai Chi, Aikido, Pilates and Feldenkrais exercises all help us feel better and more happy and alive. Take your pick!

There is *interoception* – the sensations coming from *inside* our bodies. The contentment of a full tummy, resting after you've exercised, and the delights of making love before, during and after, with someone you trust and feel safe with.

And there is *felt sense* – the signalling from our right hemisphere through our body – giving us animal insights into our own situation. Felt sense is a kind of interoception, and continuous with it, but is much more than physical. A tight shoulder is something you can feel with your hand, but its relationship to an abusive childhood (for example) makes it a profound opening into your deep mind as well. Felt sense has some distinguishing characteristics that make it unmistakable:

1. It's palpable in the body.
2. It's not purely physical – something meaningful is in there, wanting your attention.
3. It's more complex than you can put into words.
4. It begins as something very vague, almost imperceptible, but heightens when you give it your full attention.

5. If you stay with it, it will begin to set off lightbulbs of insight or forgotten memories or connections, almost always very valuable to grasp.

This is a radical idea – that our body is a thinking creature, and we can talk to it. And the fullest human potential is when we once again operate as a whole.

A Silent Retreat

Okay, here is one last story. In January of 2023, embracing a new year, I enrolled in a three-day silent retreat, in the Insight tradition of Buddhism. I figured being silent would be a worthwhile challenge for a 'gabby' person like me, and that three days wasn't too long if I hated it! The retreat was being held not far from my home, on the banks of the Tamar/kanamaluka estuary in northern Tasmania.

The teachers were Louise Taylor and Robyn Gibson, two very bright women decades younger than me. To my relief, they were kind, funny and deeply helpful, with none of the pomposity I had experienced before in meditation teachers. And we students were just eighteen in number, so we soon felt like a family.

I was coming to the crunch time of writing this book, which felt like a flock of unruly sheep in my mind that refused to be herded in one direction. What I was missing most was the actual resolution of the search – the inner experience of having two sides of one's mind getting along as they were intended. Of being actually – for even a few seconds – totally conscious. *Nobody was more surprised than I when I actually found it.*

In the meditation sessions, we were told to just notice how our thoughts would leap off on incredible random trails, and on noticing, come back to our breathing, without any self-chastisement, using such a light effort as it might take to simply move one's hand across through air in front of you. Noticing, always noticing, the sunlight, the weight of one's body on the cushion, the breeze ruffling the trees, an aching knee, quiet rumblings in one's stomach, and always the breath going in and out. We meditated sitting, but also walking softly through the bush, each step slow and measured.

What meditation is, at its very heart, is a journey into Wild Creature Mind. To learn to be there for brief moments, and then slightly longer, and then one day, almost all the time. In Buddhism this is called 'embodiment' and it acknowledges that all we have to do to escape the traps of ego and endless monkey-mind is to be aware of our own inner and outer sensations, as they arise, and our thoughts will gradually quieten and become steady and calm.

On the third day, something happened that has stayed with me. In the afternoon session of walking meditation,

walking alone and very slowly, my eye fell on a particular curved gum leaf among the millions that lay on
the ground. In that microsecond glance, I felt a kind of
sweet ache in my chest, about three inches below and to
the left of my heart. I simply noticed it with curiosity
and, as often happens when we attend to a felt sense, it
gently blossomed out and swept me with a sweet kind
of grief that was not painful, but very poignant. It felt
like I was saying goodbye to everything that gum leaves
represented – to nature, to my chosen, beloved home of
Tasmania, all the way back to childhood and what being
outdoors and 'free as a bird' had been like as a small boy
in England. Then, after a few seconds, another insight
came: I am 70, and not dead yet, but dying is a process
and I am on that road. I realised I was starting the journey
of saying goodbye to this life. The gum leaves would stay,
but I would go! I was set, by this few moments of inner
connection, on the final stage of my life. I knew what the
meaning of my next decade was to be. It was a 'Decade of
Farewell', imbued with knowing that endings have special
qualities to them. Of intensity, and of not leaving things
unsaid or undone. Of giving everything one possibly
could to those who I would leave behind. Who would
carry the torch of kindness, safeguarding nature, and
fighting the forces of greed and death that now beset us
as never before.

This book was a part of that mission and purpose. Sometimes things come together. I wasn't just teaching you, dear reader, I was *recruiting* you.

With all my heart,

Steve B.

Acknowledgements

This book brings together two different fields of science. Firstly, the neuroscience emerging in the last fifteen years, most notably in the extraordinary and acclaimed work of Iain McGilchrist. (And of Allan Schore, Daniel Siegel, and Lisa Feldman Barrett.) And the therapy/mutual-help method called 'focusing', developed by the philosopher and therapist Eugene Gendlin. My respect and gratitude to these people is beyond words.

Gendlin and McGilchrist may never have known of the other's existence, and they may well not agree with my synthesis. (Though in the foreword to Gendlin's classic book *Focusing*, Marilyn Ferguson, of the Brain Mind Bulletin, argued the same thing.)

I am rather terrified, in Iain's case, that he will see me as so oversimplifying as to be a vandal in the temple. I imagine going to his cottage door on Skye to be met with curses and hurled china, deservedly driven out into the snow. But I hope that he will see this as a humble effort to do what he is urging, to encourage a right hemisphere civilisation to arise, before the one we live in collapses.

Eugene and Mary Hendricks Gendlin are no longer alive, but left behind a widespread global network. I have talked to focusing practitioners, experienced therapy done that way, and taken a flurry of courses. But I am still really a novice in this field too. If I have gotten it wrong, then I am very sorry. I would love to hear from anyone in either field if so. Ideally I would've spent another ten years on this book. Fearful for the world, seeing the urgency and running out of cognitive powers, I didn't have that luxury.

The therapy world, however, has explored this terrain in fits and starts for over a century. After all, Freud's greatest insight had been the existence of an 'unconscious'. But there is no divide inside our brains, keeping consciousness at bay – except the great fissure that runs right down the middle. It is so patently clear that the unconscious really means the inarticulate nonverbal side of our mind. We didn't have to be 'unconscious' – Carl Jung was clear that the journey of life was to know more and more of your own hidden self, and so become more free and more fully alive. And of course Buddhism had got there thousands of years before.

A considerable team was gathered to make this book. Dr Jennifer Gardner of UTAS gave it a critical read as an educator in adult learning. She's the reason for that sparky introduction. Rosie Smith, a focusing practitioner in Perth,

Australia, gave me sessions as a therapy client, so I could experience it in action, and also made detailed comments. Robyn McKinnon, a much loved psychotherapist here in my home state, helped with how to apply Wild Creature ideas to complex trauma, and also to everyday parenting. Dr Andrew Alexander gave early emotional support as well as suggestions on tone and content. Sally Stanton sifted for the most telling quotes with her combat trained mind for context and detail. Melinda Tankard Reist, the indomitable feminist educator who has talked to tens of thousands of schoolgirls, helped me know in detail the world of the teenage girl.

Kendal and Shelley first showed me *The Master and His Emissary* without which this book would just never have happened. It's so interesting how the universe does this kind of thing.

I was lucky to meet Aurora Materia in the closing stages of the project. Aurora is very well read and experienced in neuroscience, especially neurodiversity and the limitations and lived experience of therapy, good and bad. Aurora helped verify my sense that there was huge scope to improve how psychological help is given.

Dean Yates, author of the PTSD classic *Line in the Sand*, was very helpful in the role of ritual in addressing moral injury.

Richmond Heath introduced me to TRE trembling approaches to stress release, and is a wonderful teacher.

Julie Perrin – Melbourne based writer and storyteller – generously allowed me to reproduce her story about the very special lady in the fruit shop.

The books and thinking of Ann Weiser Cornell, in Berkeley, California, have made Gendlin's work even more accessible, and her background in linguistics gave her tools to do so. Ann devised the idea of 'Something in me . . .' which is such a simple device with such huge consequence. I use this skill many times a day; we've never met, but thank you Ann for everything.

Kim McCabe, founder of the wonderful Girls Journeying Together programs around the world, guided me out of some thickets I was lost in, and gave invaluable help in teenage mental health. Kim is a person of such depth of heart that she changes your experience of being in the world.

Carole Tonkinson, formerly at Bluebird UK, gave me the freedom to write at my own pace. Ingrid Ohlsson of Pan Macmillan in Australia responded so positively to the book and stepped in to make sure it came out fast enough to be of help. Danielle Walker was a caring and enthusiastic managing editor and Libby Turner grappled with the structure which had gotten so out of hand! These three spent countless hours, made up for my cognitive deficits, and were absolute champions for the book being worth the effort. So many people are behind a book, from tree plantation to bookshop. All for you, dear reader!

My meditation teacher, Louise Taylor, helped me take that final step, to learn to live what this book teaches. My gratitude for this is beyond words. In fact, everything good is beyond words. I guess that is the point.

And always, woven through everything, to Shaaron and our tribe, for the joy and courage they all bring to life.

This book is dedicated to everyone working to turn back deadly climate change, to defeat the murderous power of the fossil fuel industry, and give the next generation a chance to survive.

Notes and Citations

Page 2: 'A radical understanding is emerging in mainstream neuroscience . . .'

McGilchrist, Iain, *The Master and His Emissary: The Divided Brain and the Making of the Western World*, 2nd edition, Yale University Press, New Haven, Connecticut, 2019.
Schore, Allan N, *Affect Regulation and the Origin of the Self: The Neurobiology of Emotional Development*, Routledge, 2015.

Page 2: 'open our hearts in hell'
This is a phrase from the work of Buddhist grief and dying counsellors Steven and Andrea Levine.

Levine, Steven and Andrea, *Meetings at the Edge*, TBS, San Francisco, 1988.

Page 8: 'Brain scientists have all kinds of technical names for this part of you'
Here is some supplementary material from Rod Tweedy's book *The Divided Therapist*:

'The right hemisphere . . . is the hemisphere that grounds us and sustains us when we start breathing . . . that underwrites the first eighteen months of our life and our earliest developmental formations . . . that supports and delivers every relationship, attachment, and embodied experience we have . . . and it is the hemisphere that empathises with our final breath.'

Cozolino, Louis, *The Neuroscience of Human Relationships: Attachment and the Developing Social Brain*, 2nd edition, W.W. Norton, New York, 2006.

Schore, Allan N, 'The Right Brain is Dominant in Psychotherapy', *Psychotherapy (Chic)*, September 2014, 51(3):388–97.

Siegel, Daniel J, *IntraConnected: MWe (Me + We) as the Integration of Self, Identity, and Belonging*, W. W. Norton, New York, 2022.

Tweedy, Rod (Ed.), *The Divided Therapist: Hemispheric Difference and Contemporary Psychotherapy*, Routledge, London and New York, 2020.

Page 9: 'Albert Einstein'

Einstein was often interviewed about how he went about making his discoveries. He always stressed that he did not use mathematics or reasoning in the first instance. Those only came into play afterwards, as a way of explaining what he had 'felt' his way towards. Einstein's following testimonial was published in Jacques Hadamard's essay (I've used italics for emphasis): 'The words or the language, as they are written or spoken, do not seem to play any role in my mechanism of thought. The above-mentioned elements are, in my case, of visual and *some of muscular type*.

Conventional words or other signs have to be sought for labori-
ously *only in a secondary stage*, when the mentioned associative
play is sufficiently established and can be reproduced at will.'

Hadamard, Jacques, *An Essay on the Psychology of Invention in
the Mathematical Field*, Dover Publications Inc., Princeton
University Press, Princeton, New Jersey, 1945.

Page 36: 'Ann Weiser Cornell'

Ann is a prolific provider of courses and YouTube talks online
at focusingresources.com. Her best-known book, *The Power of
Focusing*, is very friendly and easy read. And *Focusing in Clinical
Practice* is more technical. Don't be fooled by Ann's gentle folksy
manner, she is a breakthrough thinker in terms of how to separate
and make welcome the tangled parts that make up our selves, and
to finally make peace between them.

Cornell, Ann Weiser, *The Power of Focusing*, New Harbinger,
Oakland, California, 1996.
Cornell, Ann Weiser, *Focusing in Clinical Practice: The Essence
of Change*, W.W. Norton & Company, London, 2013.

Page 38: 'Lisa Feldman Barrett'

Lisa Feldman Barrett has written an interesting journal article on
the scientific understanding of emotion, which I highly recommend. Here is an extract:

'Laypeople and scientists alike believe that they know anger,
or sadness, or fear, when they see it. These emotions . . . are
presumed to have specific causal mechanisms in the brain and
properties that are observable (on the face, in the voice, in the

body, or in experience) – that is, they are assumed to be natural kinds . . . In this article, I review the accumulating empirical evidence that is inconsistent with the view that there are kinds of emotion with boundaries that are carved in nature. I then consider what moving beyond a natural-kind view might mean for the scientific understanding of emotion.'

Barrett, Lisa Feldman, 'Are Emotions Natural Kinds?', *Perspectives on Psychological Science*, 2006, 1:28. doi.org/10.1111/j.1745-6916.2006.00003.x

Page 40: 'Advocates of CBT have gradually begun to admit that it often fails . . .'
A good summary of this debate can be found in Oliver Burkman's article 'Therapy Wars' and you can read more in the study by Drew Westen and his colleagues. The article frames the conflict as between traditional psychoanalysis and CBT – however most clinicians see a wide and fertile ground between those extremes, and I would include somatic therapies such as Focusing as among the most fertile of all. We've known since the 1950s that therapy outcomes are based in the qualities of the therapist, independent of methods used, and as Gendlin and Rogers found, the ability of the client to 'go inside themselves'. Therapy is not a tool, it is a relationship. Wild Creature Mind approaches are an encounter between two living, breathing beings, with hearts in the game. Here is an extract from Burkman's article:

'Scholars have begun to ask pointed questions about the studies that first fuelled CBT's ascendancy . . . researchers – motivated by the desire for . . . clearly interpretable results – had often excluded up to two-thirds of potential participants, typically because they had multiple psychological problems . . . But it may mean that the people who do get studied are extremely atypical. In real life, our psychological problems are intricately embedded in our personalities. The issue you bring to therapy (depression, say) may not be the one that emerges after several sessions (for example . . . a sexual orientation you fear your family won't accept).'

Burkeman, Oliver, 'Therapy Wars: The Revenge of Freud', *The Guardian*, UK, 6 January 2016. theguardian.com/ science/2016/jan/07/therapy-wars-revenge-of-freud-cognitive- behavioural-therapy

Westen, Drew, Novotny, Catherine M, and Thompson-Brenner, Heather, 'The Empirical Status of Empirically Supported Psychotherapies: Assumptions, Findings, and Reporting in Controlled Clinical Trials', *Psychological Bulletin*, July 2004, 130(4):631–63.

Page 47: 'Dr Iain McGilchrist'
Since publishing *The Master and His Emissary*, Iain has made innumerable YouTube videos and interviews, and authored a sub-sequent and even larger book, *The Matter with Things*, about the importance of not treating ourselves, or reality, as an object to be manipulated. Exactly as Gendlin does, McGilchrist argues we are essentially relationships, not objects at all, and the cosmos is an interactive, generative, organic whole, not a machine. (Some will see a clearly spiritual aspect to this.)

McGilchrist, Iain, *The Master and His Emissary: The Divided Brain and the Making of the Western World*, 2nd edition, Yale University Press, New Haven, Connecticut, 2019.

McGilchrist, Iain, *The Matter with Things*, Perspective Press, London, 2021.

Page 107: 'Rogers has already turned the world of therapy on its head'
Rogers' second book is lively and more personal, co-written with a very right-brain enlivened colleague.

Rogers, Carl R, *On Becoming a Person: A Therapist's View of Psychotherapy*, Houghton Mifflin Company, New York, 1961.
Rogers, Carl R, and Stevens, Barry, *Person to Person: The Problem of Being Human*, Real People Press, Lafayette, California, 1967.

Page 111: 'Gendlin will develop this idea into a whole field of therapy called "focusing"'
Gendlin wrote books about focusing and founded the International Focusing Institute. The focusing community is a generous hearted worldwide network and have many free resources on their website focusing.org. You can read this excellent free summary paper by Mary Hendricks Gendlin available online: focusing. org/sites/default/files/legacy/fot/Hendricks-American-Journal-draft-81.20.06.pdf. You can also read about focusing with children, and also their approach called Thinking At The Edge – working with science thinkers and researchers in order to tap their right hemisphere knowledge to work in the vague zone between the known and the sensed but yet to be known, as Einstein described.

Gendlin, Eugene, *Focusing*, revised edition, Bantam, New York, 1981.

Gendlin, Eugene, *Focusing-Oriented Psychotherapy*, Guilford Press, New York, 1996.

Page 115: 'The right hemisphere has its own map of the body'
This of course is from Iain McGilchrist and the 2000 references in his magisterial tome! But for a quick glimpse into the astonishing world of lateralisation of the brain, this is a nice sample:

sciencedirect.com/topics/immunology-and-microbiology/right-
   hemisphere

Page 118: 'at least one in three people'
Researchers surveyed 1000 American adults and found that 49 per cent would self-identify as people pleasers. 70 per cent of women say they often go to great lengths to avoid conflict and 68 per cent say they often put other people's needs first at the expense of their own. About 52 per cent of Americans say they often feel like they can't say no when someone asks them for something. Women are more likely (55 per cent) to experience this than men (49 per cent).

Ballard, Jamie, 'Women are More Likely Than Men to Say They're a People-Pleaser, and Many Dislike Being Seen as One', YouGov, 23 August 2022.
YouGov Poll, 'People-Pleasing | YouGov Poll: June 18–21, 2022', YouGov, 22 August 2022.

Page 119: 'Mary Hendricks Gendlin, wife of Eugene Gendlin, told this story'
I quoted the core part of the story, but Mary sets it in a more philosophic and revolutionary context in the full keynote address,

easily found here: thinkinginmovement.ca/focusing/revolutionary-pause-mary-hendricks/

Page 163: 'Marta Stapert and Erik Verliefte, in their book
Focusing with Children'
This book is available from pccs-books.co.uk.

Stapert, Marta, and Verliefte, Erik, *Focusing With Children: The Art of Communicating with Children at School and at Home*, PCCS, Monmouth, 2008.

Page 173: 'suicide, which kills 700,000 people a year worldwide'
World Health Organization, 'Suicide Fact Sheet', August 2023. who.int/news-room/fact-sheets/detail/suicide

Page 179: 'Dear Eleanor'
The full advice column is featured in *The Guardian* UK and is available online.

Gordon-Smith, Eleanor, 'I Have Suppressed Hatred for My Stepmother. How Do I Have a Relationship with My Dad?', *The Guardian*, UK, 9 September 2022.

Page 202: 'Using the TRE model'
I found Richmond Health's online course a very good way to get started, and later attended a live workshop, which allowed for individual coaching and shaping of the trembling patterns for the greatest effect. His course can be found at: trecourse.com. The actual founder of TRE is Dr David Bercelli, who pioneered its use in high trauma groups around the world. You can read his book or view his website: traumaprevention.com.

Bercelli, David, *The Revolutionary Trauma Release Process: Transcend Your Toughest Times*, Namaste Publishers, Vancouver, 2008.

Page 210: 'Peter Levine's Somatic Experiencing Therapy'
Levine, Peter, *In An Unspoken Voice: How the Body Releases Trauma*, North Atlantic Books, Berkeley, California, 2010.

Page 216: 'Recent brain studies around the world have shown that during peaceful non-dreaming sleep . . .'
This is from a journal article by Megha Ghosh and her colleagues, but a more accessible summary can be found at: neuroscience-news.com/running-dreaming-brain-communication-20970/

Ghosh, Megha, et al., 'Running Speed and REM Sleep Control Two Distinct Modes of Rapid Interhemispheric Communication', *Cell Reports*, 1 July 2022, 40(1).

Page 218: 'Survivors of Auschwitz concentration camp have been studied'
Owczarski, Wojciech, 'Adaptive Nightmares of Holocaust Survivors: The Auschwitz Camp in the Former Inmates' Dreams', *Dreaming*, 2018, 28(4): 287.

Page 219: 'Dr Leslie Ellis'
Leslie Ellis is in my view the world's best clinician and writer in the area of dream and nightmare treatment. She is scholarly and has an in-depth knowledge of brain–body interaction, but writes very accessibly, with great examples of how dreams – even the most horrific – can take a client to a better waking life. Leslie generously

provides many videos and articles on her website drleslieellis.com/free-resources/. Her doctoral dissertation is called 'Stopping the Nightmare', which is on helping torture survivors to heal and progress from their nightmares. She also has a book for therapists called *A Clinician's Guide to Dream Therapy*.

Ellis, Leslie A., 'Stopping the Nightmare: An Analysis of Focusing Oriented Dream Imagery Therapy For Trauma Survivors with Repetitive Nightmares', Doctoral Dissertation, Chicago School of Professional Psychology, 25 November 2014.
Ellis, Leslie A., *A Clinician's Guide to Dream Therapy: Implementing Simple and Effective Dreamwork*, Routledge, London, 2019.

Page 227: 'The way we live now has dramatically shortened sleeping time'

Naiman, Rubin, 'Dreamless: The Silent Epidemic of REM Sleep Loss, *Annals of the New York Academy of Sciences*, 2017, 1406(1): 77–85.

Page 227: 'America's National Sleep Foundation carried out a study'

The poll is carried out annually, and you can see the results and summary findings as well as the detailed methodology here: thensf.org/sleep-in-america-polls/

Page 239: 'Elephants have wi-fi!'

I've listed below some further reading, but a good accessible summary can be found here: thecareprojectfoundation.org/a-secret-language-infrasonic-communication-in-elephants/.

Garstang, Michael, 'Long-Distance, Low-Frequency Elephant Communication', *Journal of Comparative Physiology A*, 2004, 190: 791–805.

Garstang, Michael, *Elephant Sense and Sensibility*, Academic Press, London, 2015.

Page 247: 'I was flipping pages in *The Body Keeps the Score*'

van der Kolk, Bessel, *The Body Keeps the Score: Brain, Mind, and Body in the Healing of Trauma*, Viking Press, New York, 2014.

Page 289: 'in the Insight tradition of Buddhism'

This is the Australian organisation from which Louise Taylor draws and is a member: insightmeditationaustralia.org. Other countries will have equivalent networks, but I am not familiar with those in person.

Wider Reading

For the strictly science backgrounding, the Notes and Citations on page 299 will provide a whole universe to explore. But if you wish to look from a philosophical perspective, two outstanding books about the importance of seeing ourselves as animals are the classic *Beast and Man: The Roots of Human Nature* by Mary Midgeley (1979) and the brand-new book that has been widely acclaimed *How to Be Animal: A New History of What It Means to Be Human* by Melanie Challenger (2023).

For a special treat, an extraordinary novel that captured me like no other, read this fictional story on the experiential world of a wild animal: *A Black Fox Running* by Brian Carter (2018 edition).